WHAT PEOPLE ARE SAYING ABOUT

A PATH OF JOY

Paramananda writes with a lighthearted clarity about the pathless path to freedom. As he shares from his own experience, and expresses from beyond all experience, his words will resonate with your own knowing and touch you deeply. Enjoy the ride.

Unmani, author of *Die to Love*

You have created a fun, light-hearted, easy-to-read, yet powerful invitation to enlightenment. The principles you teach are right on and will bring increasing moments of awakening to all who practice them. You have evolved from a determined seeker and great comedian to a wise and effective teacher – a wonderful expression of your own spiritual transformation along the Path of Joy.

John C. Robinson, Ph.D., D.Min., author of *The Three Secrets of Aging, Bedtime Stories for Elders, What Aging Men Want*

Paramananda's new book offers a kaleidoscope of spiritual teachings and insights that spark self enquiry on a myriad of levels. You really feel that he is sitting with you one-on-one as his clear wisdom envelops you and guides to your own joyful path to freedom.

Lawrence Ellyard, author of *Reiki Meditations '*   ` and *The Spirit of Water*

Paramananda has written a gem of a book   und. Finding joy in each moment we are   een so attainable.

Richard A Singer Jr., author of   *.he Present Moment*

A Path of Joy is a meaningful yet light-hearted book that brings joy and insight to the spiritual journey. With grace and humor, Paramananda Ishaya reminds us that we have permission to think less and enjoy more. We don't really have to "know" anything; we can gently remove the concepts, and just settle back into the silence and stillness that has been with us all along.

Dee Willock, author of *Falling Into Easy: Help For Those Who Can't Meditate*

Paramananda has heard the silence and experienced the bliss. This book takes the reader to the core of the non-dual reality and brilliantly reminds the seeker not to take it all too seriously otherwise you make the mistake of seeking that which you already are.

Maurice Anslow, author of *I am Brahman*

A Path of Joy takes a light hearted look at a personal spiritual journey and the ancient wisdoms and teachings encountered on the way. Paramananda cleverly distills those teachings into a very simple but potent form that can be easily applied to modern day living. He encourages us all to embrace the silence that we might discover our true nature and experience a life of joyful living.

Lucy O'Hagan, Therapist, Acupuncturist and author of *Beyond The Here and Now*

A Path of Joy

Popping into Freedom

A Path of Joy

Popping into Freedom

Paramananda Ishaya

MANTRA
BOOKS

Winchester, UK
Washington, USA

First published by Mantra Books, 2014

Mantra Books is an imprint of John Hunt Publishing Ltd., Laurel House, Station Approach, Alresford, Hants, SO24 9JH, UK

office1@jhpbooks.net

www.johnhuntpublishing.com

www.mantra-books.net

For distributor details and how to order please visit the 'Ordering' section on our website.

Text copyright: Paramananda Ishaya 2013

ISBN: 978 1 78279 323 6

A CIP catalogue record for this book is available from the British Library.

Design: Stuart Davies

www.stuartdaviesart.com

Cover: Bhaya Ishaya

Printed and bound by CPI Group (UK) Ltd, Croydon, CR0 4YY

We operate a distinctive and ethical publishing philosophy in all areas of our business, from our global network of authors to production and worldwide distribution.

CONTENTS

Humanity takes itself too seriously. It is the world's original sin. If the cave-man had known how to laugh, History would have been different.
— Oscar Wilde, The Picture of Dorian Gray

The monkeys solved the puzzle simply because they found it gratifying to solve puzzles. They enjoyed it. The joy of the task was its own reward.
— Daniel H. Pink, Drive: The Surprising Truth About What Motivates Us

To Maharishi Krishnananda Ishaya

Foreword

I first met Paramananda in the early 1990s in White Rock, a town some 30 minutes outside of Vancouver, Canada. I was visiting some colleagues who were running meditation and consciousness courses in the area. They had some students over at their house on the day I arrived, one of which was a scruffy little guy, all dressed in white.

Every now and again in this crazy dance of life, you meet someone who you feel you have known forever. This guy was one of those for me. In fact, many of my colleagues felt the same way.

Two things immediately struck me about him: The first was his obvious desire for spiritual experience, and for waking up from his dream of separation and limitation. He was so totally attentive to all of the teachers around him, listening to what they said and watching their every move.

It was also obvious he had read a lot about spiritual discovery. Every conversation with him was infused with all of the right concepts about consciousness and awakening, but none of the experience. Like many on a "spiritual path," his mind had convinced him that if it sounded true and "enlightened," and he understood it, then it must have become his experience.

The other thing that struck me about him was a deep and constantly underlying nervous tension. He was so uncomfortable in his own skin, and in trying to be all the right things for everyone in his world, he had lost himself completely.

This is in no way meant to portray Paramananda as a fool, quite the opposite actually. In one way or another, we all have done this; we have all lost ourselves. We have taken the light and beauty of who we truly are and covered it in a mask that we believe is a more appropriate face to show the world.

For the rare few who realise this, most of the available paths promising Self-discovery give us little more than concepts and beliefs about our true nature. What is so rare on this planet is a path that will allow the student to rise beyond the negative and limiting patterns of the mind to directly experience the beauty and perfect innocence of their true self.

That is what makes this book so different to most. This book is written by a guy who has gone beyond those patterns which kept him small and afraid and who has become a direct expression of his divinity.

The anxious and limited Paramananda is gone, and what is left is what was always there for those with the eyes to see: compassionate, loving, radiating bliss, alive, supremely funny and above all, wise in a way that can only come from an intimate and genuine experience.

There are so few people who can teach and share about true freedom from their own direct experience. That is why so few paths can lead a student into the magical realm of presence that exists beyond the chatter of the linear mind. Paramananda is one of those rare beings. It is not possible to know freedom and still present it as difficult, because it is the ultimate simplicity. It is not possible to experience pure consciousness and still present it as a need to fix yourself to be worthy of it, because it requires nothing of you. It is not possible to know the Silent all-ness that you are and still take anything seriously at all, because in that state, all that remains is bliss. Paramananda is a Sanskrit name that means "Highest Bliss," and he is absolutely that.

This book reflects him perfectly and carries all of those qualities to the reader. To know Paramananda is to know that true joy and freedom from limitation are not only possible, but also easy. May you be inspired by the book to seek that realisation for yourself and to know that you can laugh all the way there!

Jai Isham Ishvaram

Narain Ishaya
Best selling author of Chit Happens – A Guide to Discovering Divinity

Acknowledgements

To the Ishayas, all your praise and encouragement to keep writing these little kernels gave me the passion and motivation to keep going until the book was completed. This work happened because of you, and for that I am forever grateful.

To Shanti, (Mi Amor), thanks for all your love and support and for making me laugh so much. I am so lucky to have you in my life.

To Caroline Kaiser, your help in editing the structure of the manuscript was nothing short of amazing. Thank you.

To Mom, you are the sweetest mom I could ask for, and I am glad I chose you! Thanks for always being here for me, especially when I was going crazy.

To Dad, thanks for coming back into my life to save me. You are an inspiration.

Introduction

My name is Paramananda, but you can call me "P" or "sweet P."

I was born as Rick de Champlain in Cowtown—Calgary, Alberta, Canada. I lived with my mother, Suzanne, until I was five years old, and then we moved to Edmonton, Alberta, with my stepfather, Dave. At the age of twelve, I was living in St. Albert (a smaller town near Edmonton) when I moved back to Calgary to live with my father, who is another Rick or Rick Sr. Today I live

in an area of Vancouver called Kitsilano with my beautiful girlfriend, Shanti.

After looking for a solution to anxiety in my life, I learned some meditation techniques that helped me experience peace. I treasured them intensely for the simple reason that they worked. Until I found them, my life was full of anxiety, pain, and fear, and I was desperate for a solution.

Ironically, my life before meditation looked wonderful from the outside. I had everything I wanted, including a well-paid job, a nice house, a car, great friends, a loving girlfriend, and a nice relationship with my parents. I was, however, stuck in a self-absorbed, seemingly hopeless state of anxiety with no possibility of a silver lining.

Meditation gave me a twenty-four-hour-a-day choice. I finally could choose the peace of Silence over the pain of nonstop thinking about myself all the time. Before meditation, I could not really say I had a choice in the matter—I was indeed a victim!

The life of Paramananda looks pretty ordinary from the outside, maybe even a little boring to some. My average day looks like this: I get up and make coffee (the most important part of the day) and have some granola. I practise meditation; I go to work at a construction site in the Vancouver area and do my job. I come home and spend time with my lovely girlfriend, and then we watch our favourite TV series and go to bed. Repeat.

The surprise is that this is not an accurate description of the life of P, despite what it looks like to me or the rest of the world! The surprise is that an infinite aliveness exists simultaneously as my life occurs. Indeed, there is only this infinite surprise.

How I appear in the world is a unique expression. I did not choose this expression—I can't help being as good-looking as I am, nor can I help getting better looking every day; it is just happening that way. This expression can be labelled and identified in a variety of ways, yet none of these are ultimately true (except for being good-looking). That they are not true is absolutely liberating.

My expression of myself is generally content and consistently joyful, but it does get grumpy, annoyed, frustrated, sad, and anxious; it has all the characteristics of the average Joe. There is nothing in the human condition that is beyond my expression.

But I have a secret. Shhhhh! Don't tell anyone, or I might have to go back to see a psychiatrist again. The secret is that none of these traits have anything to do with what I am; they do not define me. These traits are not wrapped around a separate centre called me. All these events only seem to happen to me as a separate individual. They are experienced as phenomena within the aliveness of life. This surprise is an absolutely amazing mystery.

Equally amazing is that life functions quite well like this. In fact, life is much easier and simpler from this unknown place of self. When the average Joe calls my name, I don't stare at him as if to say, "There's no one here." I respond and come over because he is calling *my* name. In our conversation, Joe might think that he's talking to me, but he's talking to a mystery. Our identities are just labels for this surprise mystery. There is an intense joy in living in that aliveness.

Earlier on the spiritual path, I had the desire to write a book. I remember specifically reflecting on the suffering in the world and feeling that I was not alone. My heart yearned to help alleviate this massive suffering in some way, yet I felt completely inadequate to the task. After all, what could I offer when I was in such a mess? I would imagine that I had attained some great wisdom I could share with the world. At times I actually believed I had attained it even though I was still suffering.

Had I written a book at that time, it would have been called something like *How to Use the Extraterrestrials and Angels to Anchor and Activate Cosmic Light into your Chakra System and Climb your Way up the 360 Levels to God.* What I called wisdom was actually the collection of things I had read about at the New Age book store down the block.

This book started as a series of weekly emails I was sending to the teachers of The Bright Path. As they became longer and more frequent, I decided to compile them into a book and expand on them. The topics contained here are an invitation to explore what you are.

To discover the difference between reality and unreality through direct experience is what I call true spirituality. The simple and fundamental truth cannot be destroyed or changed but only revealed through seeing the false as false. Liberation is certain because truth *is truth*. Experiencing this is everything.

In my own experience, I have found that the truth can be expressed conceptually through a variety of angels and angles, which is why one of my favourite things to do is to listen to different teachers as they share the stillness and what liberation is to them. This includes the amazing teachers of The Bright Path but also teachers of other paths or no paths at all.

The path of joy is a gift that, once truly seen, is instantly treasured because it has no end. It automatically transcends time and space since it is eternal. In this sense it could be called *"no path of joy,"* since you are in truth already sitting or standing in eternity as you read these words.

There is no limit to the joy and aliveness of exploring this path. It is my wish that, as you read these words, you will rediscover that eternal path of joy. I make the assumption that you prefer a path of joy to a path of pain since you are reading this.

These descriptions are from self-discoveries that unfolded before, during, and after time spent in retreats with fellow teachers and friends, as well as with the teacher who originally taught me the meditation I continue to practise today. This teacher is the inspiration behind the book and the path of joy.

Each topic is an invitation to explore the mystery of what is absolute and beyond ideas. In the end, this book can give you nothing but pointers and is only one of a million such pointers in life. Take advantage of all these nudges and winks and enjoy the greatest and only adventure there is!

Cheers to the mystery.

The Popcorn Effect

I'm not trying to butter you up when I say that you are just like popcorn!

Darwin had it wrong; we are more closely related to popcorn than we are to monkeys. Maybe we act like monkeys because we are similar genetically, but energetically we pop like popcorn.

What does this energetic pop feel like? What is it like to be Popcorn jumping out of the bucket?

This popping is fully coming into the aliveness of all there is. Then we transcend that which we think we are in order to see what we are. It could be an intense surge of bliss, a calm soothing peace or an ocean of Love. It can even appear as the "no big deal" of nothingness. However it comes to you, it is certain to be a coming into what you truly are!

Looking back at my own experience I see that it has been a combination of these. I could not predict what the next pop would look like: Peace, Stillness, Joy... this is living on the edge of aliveness. The more you stay on this edge, the more points you get until the universe gives you a frequent popper card, giving you all the free benefits of self-discovery.

For some this Pop can be an inspiration or an insight (In sight) in which we see into the Heart and through the Story of separation. This is the flowering of wisdom. The beauty of this pop is that it is not a single one-time event. Can you imagine if that was all there was? Okay I popped, now what? The great news is that this popping adventure is eternal and never ending in its popping. Each pop is like a gift that keeps filling us up with endless joy. The infinite is always turned on inviting us to see into this ancient and fresh mystery. To see this is popping into freedom.

Of course, we are also consumers of popcorn. When we want to sit down and enjoy a movie, we go grab the bowl of popcorn and start munching away. When the infinite wants to enjoy the show, it munches on us just like popcorn. When we are ready to Pop and our kernel is about to explode, the silence starts chewing on everything we think we are. The Divine opens up to taste all that we appear to be, whether good or bad. It chews and chews enjoying the flavour we have, and then eventually it swallows it all up in one big gulp. As we get eaten up the show gets more and more enjoyable for the Self and also for us. This is the essence of being out of the way so that what remains can relax and enjoy the show. The infinite is also not only the ultimate popcorn maker but the ultimate enjoyer of popcorn and out of love for the show, provides us with everything that we need to pop.

This popping effect is happening right now as more of us discover the simplicity of the path of joy. Some have already popped, some are in the process of popping, and some will pop one day. Once you pop, you just can't stop; this popping is uncontrollable once set in motion. It is not hot air, however, but stillness that brings about this awakening or popping. The stillness of being is all we need to reach the highest bliss. There is little we can do except keep emptying our buckets and staying receptive to the mystery underlying the popcorn effect.

To make popcorn, you need kernels and a popcorn maker. To make freedom, all you need is you and silence. Silence is all you need to pop—it's that easy. But this ancient simple path has apparently remained hidden by modern complexity. Nothing has changed what is obvious, yet as if by coincidence, our consciousness has identified with being a separate character in the show. What this means is that the spirit of our true nature is already free from being caught up in the drama happening on the screen of life. Yet it does not see this because it is staring in the opposite direction. In other words, it is totally absorbed in being the character (like any good actor would do) and has completely forgotten that it is only a role. It thinks that the character and everything that dresses it up in the role belong to it. It has forgotten that it is only one tiny role in an infinite show. Before that identification, there was only freedom or nothing separate for consciousness to identify with. The show must go on; however, the question is only about how to proceed or how to direct the attention.

To wake up is to recognise that nothing is in the way of freedom and that the veil of identity is actually fragile and disappears thousands of times during the day. To be liberated is to see that there is only concept-free freedom. Freedom is free of all notions of liberation and limitation. Anything we can conceive of in our heads about what we are is an idea only. What remains when we abandon all conceptualising in favour of this simple emptiness is the absolute truth.

How can we recognise the natural way of being?

There is no such thing as popcorn without the kernel. We need the seed or desire to Pop! It is as simple as wanting to Pop. How can you pop if you are not even in the pot? The problem is that people talk about wanting peace, freedom and contentment in their lives, but they really don't. They will argue with you on this, but the bottom line is that they have other priorities. The question is: what do you want? You, reading this right now! Do you have something in mind?

Okay, now that you have your kernel, the rest is all about how I can get your kernel to pop. The simple answer is Silence. Don't worry; I won't leave you hanging on the how question; just keep exploring and the kernel will pop on its own as long as you are clear on what you want. That is your job. My job is the how; let me worry about that for you. What you want is step one, to get to the Zen of How; just keep reading and don't cheat and skip to the end, okay?

You know how uncontrollable making popcorn can be, and much depends on your expertise and technique. You watch the oil bubble or the hot air push up at the kernels as they eagerly wait to pop. The popping begins as they start bouncing and jumping around. Then you get closer, thinking you're done as the pops occur seconds apart. You take the lid off and *pop!* You scream as they explode, shooting all over the place. Finally, you have what you need to relax and enjoy the show.

In the same way you need hot air for popcorn, you need the silence of being to enjoy the movie of life. The plain truth is, we don't really have a life without silence, which is the source of life, awakening, and enjoyment. The path of joy is being able to enjoy watching the movie without being caught up in the drama happening in it. This is the feature presentation, and you are the star. What is your character going to do next?

Aliveness awaits anyone willing to see through the stories we have wrapped around our lives. These include noble stories like the search for peace, fulfillment, and enlightenment. Ironically, our ideas of spirituality and freedom can keep us from the liberation we seek, leaving us with the sense that something is missing. Instead of being liberated, we keep wandering around the movie set in circles looking for the exit. Each exit sign, however, leads to another set, which leads to another exit sign. We finally find ourselves in a house of mirrors, unable to shake off continually seeking one thing after another. We are unable to discern what we are because we think we can find it in a reflection, but all the reflections reveal are more reflections.

Can waking up to the truth be as simple as popcorn popping? Absolutely *yes!* If it is not that simple, then the simplicity of what we are and the path to freedom are being clouded by ideas. But popping is spontaneously happening all around you. Can you see it? It is happening now as you read these words. It is happening within the totality of what you are. It is an energetic and silent *pop!*

There is a cosmic joke going around, and you can hear a silent, sweet laughter. The angels are laughing. We are the joke, and jokes aren't very funny when we do not get them. Enlightenment is like a joke that takes you awhile to get. Has it ever taken a while for something to click? I admit I can be a little slow sometimes, and every once in while I'll be walking on the sidewalk past a coffee shop and suddenly get it, something so embarrassingly obvious that was staring me in the face the whole time. Why didn't I see it! Duh! In the same way, when we get out of the way, freedom, like popcorn, jumps out at us and pops.

What we are is so normal, ordinary, and obvious that it is a laugh that everyone is not totally aware of this. The truth is a great mystery because it cannot be seen by looking outside ourselves but by seeing the mystery already happening within us. It is a mystery because it is unknown. The mind can know many things but cannot know the silence. A path of joy takes the "cosmic explorer" into the unknown, and in absolute bliss, unravels the wonder of being and the awe of silent nothingness.

The only honest answer to what you are is, "I don't know." What you are is not an object. What you appear to be as a separate person most certainly is an object when viewed from the ultimate subjectivity which is in the realm of the unknown. The mind can know things about you and can analyse and ponder, yet it cannot know its own absence.

It is because we take our spiritual growth so seriously that our essence remains obscure. This seriousness can make the journey seem long and difficult. Let's be clear right off the bat—the path of joy takes commitment but not seriousness. The silence is unbounded bliss—an eternal, alive popping. It's an unending, joyful exploration that doesn't just end in joy but begins in it.

We can learn a lot from popcorn and those humans who have popped before us. Who was the first? Have you ever watched popcorn pop? It is hard to say who was first or the best, but does it really matter if it was Little Buddha or Baby Jesus? The popcorn effect is happening right now, and the pot is warm with the fire of stillness. Jump in—you will love it!

The effect of popping is swift because it does not recognise anything but what is eternal and true. You are not just a separate kernel popping; the whole popcorn effect is happening within what you are. That is how big you are! You are a master popper.

As we jump or are tossed into the fire and shaken up, some of us resist and get burnt, or we try so hard we get tossed out prematurely. At other times we let go and allow the popping to happen naturally. The path of joy is a rediscovery of the swift way to pop. All it takes is a willingness to jump. But ask yourself whether you are not already in the pot. Once you are, the magic of silence does the rest. Can it really be as simple as that?

The Kernels

Out of silence springs infinite expressions of being. Each of these expressions is alive and fully rooted in the self. They act like a bridge between nothing and everything. These kernels of truth are expressed in many ways and are like different flavours of popcorn. Out of all these flavours, these expressions are only a small sample taste. You don't have to go far to find them—they are in your own direct experience. I encourage you to see these little kernels.

All popcorn tastes good, yet each of us has our favourite flavours. When we share a particular flavour, it enlivens the popcorn effect. As you are reading, this alive sharing looks like the words and spaces appearing on the page. The magic is in the context underlying what appears on this page. The magic is in what appears within you (you being the context, not the content). This is the infinite mystery of resonance.

Each facet of expression is intimately linked with its source, and like a tuning fork, it calls us home to the source of its vibration. In the silence we are connected to this source. We take this journey together, both you and me and the rest of humanity. Since there is already only unity, the path to it is beyond the limits of time, space, and what seems to separate us from the whole. Energetically, we feel this unity beyond the intellect in the quiet space where nothing moves. Ultimately, everything comes back to stillness, and each facet, like a ray of sunlight, takes us back home into the sun.

Before I continue, I have one thing to ask of you. If you do only this, I promise your life will become more miraculous and enjoyable than ever. Even if you put this book down and don't read another sentence, take this one piece of advice with you. *Don't take anything seriously!* Don't take me seriously, but most of all, don't take yourself seriously! Any difficulty in life always comes from taking yourself too seriously because you are thinking and conceptualising. There is nothing wrong with thinking, but it can be bad for your health and dangerous to your peace. It's useful to remember that thinking too much is a good sign you are taking something too seriously. When you see this happening, it becomes possible to make a different choice.

I am not telling you to not be responsible—not to pay rent or feed your cat. You can pay taxes, eat well, go to work, and live with incredible fluidity without taking things seriously. Each day, try to take life less seriously than the day before. If you run into trouble because you are smiling too much or laughing at a funeral, just pretend to be serious. Pretending will work fine. That is what I do at work; I pretend that I am serious, and I am getting better at it. I even put a frown on my face to fit in. Remember the words of the great sage, Manyu: "It's not about how you feel... it's about how you look."

Manyu is a wise yet very funny teacher I had the pleasure of spending time with him at a meditation retreat. He is from Las Vegas, and if you pictured him as a loud, crazy, big Elvis with big sunglasses and a big smile, you would not be far off. One day I was busy thinking and feeling not very cheerful when I heard him scream loudly, "Oh my God!"

I came running to see what had happened. He was looking in a mirror, looking shocked. "What happened?" I said.

He turned to me slowly with his big smile and said, "I just get better looking every day!"

I laughed, and all my pain vanished instantly. He was one of the most amazing teachers I've ever met; he was totally serious about God, yet not very serious about anything else. His approach to starting out the game of spirit was to say, "Just pretend."

Remember, we are just like characters in a movie. We kick back with a box of popcorn, watching ourselves trip and fall over, spilling popcorn over someone's head and laughing the whole time. The silence is watching and enjoying our character, even if it's a bad movie. If the Source of Life doesn't take us seriously, why should we? But we are so caught up in the characters playing the roles that we forget to enjoy the movie. How we live and where we come from sets up an energetic field that either raises or lowers consciousness. The source of consciousness itself doesn't change, but what makes all the difference is how we live and experience our own life. This, in turn, affects those closest to us and the world around us; hence we have the popcorn effect.

Throughout our adventure we will explore how to loosen the grip that seriousness has on our journey and reveal the truth of being, which never in eternity took a single thought, feeling, or action seriously; it only appears that way in time and space to the separate individual.

I don't wish to add another concept to our mental baggage; however, my observations are based on direct experience of the essential nature, which is the aliveness of infinite silence. The job is not over until you can lose yourself in that essential truth. You don't have to wait—just start practising (pretending) *not taking anything seriously*. Especially this. If you can't do that, staying alert and open will work fine. Actually forget all that and just keep emptying the bucket of concepts.

Despite any apparent difference in flavours, one thing remains the same throughout eternity in every human being in all cultures regardless of belief and programming: the nothingness of *silence*. The silence *never changes*, yet changes appear to happen within it. The silence *never moves*, though movement can appear to happen. The silence is the ultimate foundation of everything, the source of life, and the foundation of enlightenment. Enlightenment means dissolving in the silence through attention and getting what the heart desires by not taking life seriously. That's the long way to say *popping*!

It is difficult to describe, yet very easy to experience. That which you are *is* the experiencing of it. The silence is a natural experience. You have already experienced it directly thousands of times in your life! You were not aware of how significant it was because it was so familiar to you. One of the first comments people make when they become aware of the significance of the silence is, "No way—this is it? It can't be this simple!" Yet there it is in front of your face (actually shining out of your face). Fully waking up is like this as well—a great and mighty cosmic "duh!"

I like to explain it in that way, but ancient texts like the Vedas talk about non-duality or "not two." In physics, reality is understood to be infinite, so everything is connected as one big self. There is nothing but this one. This is just a concept, however, until we reach a point in consciousness where we are holding nothing at all (including our little self). Reaching this is the experience of the silence with no added ingredients. If it is true that there is only one and you are that one, how much effort would it take to really be yourself—that is, the only self that exists? In theory it would take exactly *zero* effort. But let's find out for ourselves instead of talking about it.

If you bought enlightenment in a bottle at 7-Eleven, the ingredients on the label would say, "Contains nothing." You would be paying for a bottle of nothing! All the other qualities are hidden within it and magically appear from this nothingness. If you were to drink it, what would happen? Nothing. Nothing would happen because you are already free. Nothing needs to be added to you at all. Enlightenment seems difficult because we are trying to add something to nothing, which adds confusion to nothing.

This nothing only appears empty, dull, and boring for one reason: it has remained unexplored. But infinite treasures lie there in its silence. In it is a never-ending infinite expression of joy.

The silence is the most obvious and valuable thing in the world and also the most undervalued. It is easy to dismiss nothingness because it isn't seen for what it is. As we move along the spiritual path, we are naturally drawn to what will allow us to fulfil our highest desire. Ultimately, as our desires become more refined, what we desire is the *one*—the whole enchilada, not just the tortilla shell. Most of us are satisfied with the genetically modified tortilla shell because everyone is chewing on one. Stop chewing on plastic and taste Heaven.

It doesn't matter what we call Heaven—God, Buddha, self, chocolate, or silence. Also, it doesn't matter what we call this path of return to joy—meditation, grace, or surrender. I often use the terms silence, nothingness, and path of joy, but let's try not to take these terms seriously.

The mind wants to figure out the meaning of these terms, which is perfectly fine. That's what it does, and we will let it continue. We will do our best to give the intellect enough to chew on, and maybe it will let go and have an *a-ha* or two. Allow the curiosity to be there and question it all. After all, this is about your self-discovery. It doesn't matter which level of consciousness we have reached or how enlightened we think we are; the silence remains alert and open to everything and invites us to play with self-exploration. In the end, this playing is all that is happening anyway.

Even when we are stuck and confused, the silence allows us that experience. Consciousness loves to play and discover itself even if the mind thinks it understands. It is always enlivening to share the silence and let go of this position and that position. The most conscious people on the planet are humble enough to see what they are holding onto; they even get excited when they see it. Why? The infinite is very big, and to see what limits the fullness of that is inspiring.

We are going to explore the silence together energetically. We have come together in this way to do just that. What else could we want? Exploring it is pure magic. It's no accident you got to this point in your life, and good job you made it this far! Are you ready for even more magic?

We can resonate with the silence in many ways. One way is through a teaching, teacher, or those we share the same energy of truth with. The self is like a divine magnet, pulling us more and more as we bring the attention of the mind and the heart into the infinite.

Self-exploration is all about an energetic resonance with what is. The silence is the absolute, void of any story or quality, complete, unmoving, and non-dual. The apparent paradox is that the transparent and unchanging self allows for an infinite variety of flavours while having no flavour or quality at all. It is a transparent canvas for all colours to dance upon. When we add red colouring to a glass of water, it appears red, yet it is clear water in essence. When we add ideas and concepts into nothingness, we shade its appearance as well. It's just plain old kindergarten science. Thank God it is easier to see the difference between a concept and its source than it is to take the red out of the water. Go ahead and try!

The more we come to realise the stillness, the more doors open up for us to play with the infinite treasure of riches that have been overlooked throughout time. We cannot see the perfection of our world simply because we have not made a distinction between the real (eternal) and the unreal (time). This distinction is the greatest realisation we can make because it leads to the highest fulfillment.

Jesus said that unless we are like children, we cannot enter the kingdom of Heaven. As children, we knew how to play because we had not yet forgotten our innocence. Silence enables us to return to playing.

Like kernels that pop into popcorn, we are each divine expressions of God. The fulfillment of each and every expression is the sacred right of every human on the planet and in the universe. I am not just blowing hot air here. What are you waiting for? Plug in the popcorn maker and turn it on!

Let the cosmic adventure begin; strap on your cosmic explorer helmets, and let's shoot to the stars.

Finding the Path

Eternal Peace

Nothing real can be threatened. Nothing unreal exists. Herein lies the Peace of God.

—*A Course in Miracles*

What is it that apparently obscures the reality of peace? What is your story?

When I first started to experience what I now call peace, it felt like an ease I couldn't explain. Looking back, I see it as a peace that began filling up every area of my life. It started to happen during the first few months after I started using the new meditation techniques I learned in Vancouver during a weekend retreat. Something definitely different was happening as I practised, most noticeably at work. All I was doing was repeating phrases of truth my teachers called attitudes whenever I could remember. What was amazing was that I was doing this with my eyes open all day and whenever I wanted. The teacher had told me I should use the technique often and with my eyes open to reduce the amount of incoming stress.

Stress was a big deal for me during the workday. The pull to go inward and rest became so strong that I would find one or two minutes every once in a while and sneak off to practise with my eyes closed. If you can't find an old storage closet, then the bathroom will work nicely. (Nobody bothers you there, hopefully.) At the time I was working in a plastics factory, and I found an abandoned old shower with a chair in it. One day I was completely blissed out while meditating in that shower when my boss came in and busted me. He said, "What are you doing?" I told him I was just taking a nap. Good thing it was on a night shift, so falling asleep wasn't that out of the ordinary.

Those little (or big) chunks of time are an investment in your eternal peace. They are precious moments where you can honestly say you did not waste your time. The only thing permanent is this peace, since everything else comes and goes. That is not just a nice idea but the way things actually work.

Why not invest in what doesn't change? This is literally the *most* important thing you can do for yourself, and more than that, for everyone around you, me included. When you focus on peace, you take a load off our backs. I don't have to worry so much about you anymore.

Before I started to make that investment, I would wake up to my alarm every day with suicidal feelings; I was praying to die, begging for some relief. The thought of getting up was awful. Just before waking was peace—the peace of sleep that I craved because I disappeared into the sweet abyss of nothingness. What if you could have this peace of sleep in the waking state?

Just being conscious made me angry; I didn't want to wake up and face the world. (These are just normal feelings in the morning—I am sure you know those grumpy people who need their coffee.) Instead of staying identified with the peace of sleep, my consciousness grabbed onto the same familiar thoughts. What made getting up difficult was this habit of grabby-ness, which turned into crabbiness.

Then one day a miracle happened! When the alarm went off, I did not want to kill myself. I was not as bothered by those familiar sensations and the thoughts of depression. They were there but seemed somehow less relevant now. I began my morning with meditation attitudes and a hit of coffee, and I was off on the path of joy. I have had many miracles happen since that weekend retreat, but this was one of the most amazing and most welcome ones ever. Thanks universe, for sending me those meditation teachers!

Little miracles happen when we value peace in our lives. I truly believe they began to happen because of my intense desire and commitment to meditation. At the time I didn't even recognise what the silence was or how to focus attention on it. That didn't matter at all! The teachers told me that introducing the technique into my life would automatically take me there. Now I had proof that it was working, so I wanted to see how far I could go with it. I started to use it whenever I remembered to. As I became aware I had to pee in the middle of the night, bam, I would use it and then get up to go to the bathroom. More peace! Where was the end? How much more peace could I experience? How much easier could life get? The key was to make it a fun game.

I started to be aware of myself living, getting up, going to work, and "doing the routine" as if I was witnessing everything happen. Suddenly, the puppet was my friend; some days it was like Elmo, and others it was like Oscar the Grouch. Life seemed easier than ever. I really didn't know what was happening, but looking back now, I see that I focused less attention on little me, and a natural witnessing began unfolding. To me that was proof enough that the path of joy was working, so I kept up my practice, especially with my eyes open. The only difficulty I encountered was trying to remember to look "normal" – I had to appear unhappy because I was at a job I hated.

Unknowingly, I would forget my serious face and walk around like a smiling idiot, getting comments like, "Why the hell are you smiling?" or "What are you so happy about – are you high?" Oops – engage and activate serious work face now! Pretend you are a normal person who hates his job like everyone else. The funny thing was, I still didn't like my job at all (especially the swing shift), but the peace was attracting me more than the dislike. It seemed as though I enjoyed my job more, but really I was falling in love with the silence and the path of joy. It didn't matter what I was doing anymore; I was simply happier.

I have always had this fear of doing the wrong thing or getting in trouble. As consciousness expands, the universe tends to reflect your inner experience on the outside more quickly. One day at work, we were preparing like crazy for an open house with the corporate heads who were on their way to see the operation. By accident I drove a forklift through the window of the control office. With shocked people staring at me, all I could do was remember to silently use the meditation technique while I waited for the boss's hammer to hit me. Strangely enough, I did not worry because there was nothing else I could do. Peace like I've never had surrounded and protected me. When the boss came, he didn't yell at me or freak out. (He was famous for yelling.) With ease he carried on, called a repair guy, and got the window fixed without any drama. Could life be this easy? Would it have even mattered if he'd yelled at me, proving that indeed I was a bad boy?

We sit in the middle of the kingdom of Heaven waiting to see the beauty and wonder. Playing the waiting game isn't fun, yet we get a secret reward by continuing to delay what is already the case now. We get to continually prove that we aren't ready for peace because... blah, blah, blah. Yes, I've heard it all before. It's as if we cover our eyes in denial, not being totally willing to see, though maybe we take just a quick peek. We tell ourselves we're almost ready, almost there, and that we have just one more thing to let go of. Our journey and the world around us tend to support this position of waiting. There are so many rationalisations for waiting.

Our excuses are validated because the "I don't deserve it" feeling is too strong for us to really see the fullness of our nature. And so the excuses go on. There is no rule that says we have to wait. But there is no rule that says we have to wait for our story to vanish either. In fact, who wrote these rules, and where is this rule book?

As the peace became more common, I began to experience strange contradictions. I was told that was normal. When I went to a longer retreat, I was totally absorbed in stillness, joy, and peace—most of the time. Bliss radiated from my eyes, yet I was simultaneously depressed, paranoid, anxious, and scared of everything. What? Does this make sense? I was walking around in the kingdom of Heaven while listening to the lies in my head. There were two worlds going on at the same time. How strange this contrast between reality and fantasy was! I was sick of everyone telling me how well I was doing and praising me. I was not doing well at all—couldn't they see that? I must have been the greatest actor in the world.

Frustrated, I looked at myself in the mirror and thought, "You're no good. You'll never get there—you're sad and pathetic." But I also saw the biggest smile; I looked so happy and blissed out. What was wrong with me? No wonder people were so confused. "Damn it, I'm depressed! Nobody will believe me if I look so happy!"

It was as if my body was completely ignoring my mind and favouring the peace of the stillness over my thoughts of depression. This happiness was what people saw, not what I was thinking. I thought, "How nice of them to say nice things to me." Later I remember being told that we tend to see the beauty in others before we see it in ourselves. Now I know I am not just a beautiful face.

The peace or ease we seek is already happening within us before we seek it. Our story may continue and be seen clearly in light of what we are. We see it for what it is because of the contrast. Before we listen to the story, is it really true that peace is not here, or are we just fascinated with ourselves and our story?

Our story is very important to us because it gives us a reason why we don't have peace in our lives. If peace is more important to you than the story, then who cares why? On the path of joy, sometimes a stress release happens to clear out some of the gunk that has built up in our nervous systems. It is our job as warriors of bliss to let it go—both the story and the gunk. This process is natural if we allow it. If we choose to favour the story over the peace, then we turn off the popcorn maker before the kernels get a chance to pop. We need the silence of being to pop!

As we lose ourselves in the silence, our nervous systems shake off anything that is not for the highest good. This is part of the popcorn effect. As we let it go, we make it easier for the next kernel to pop. We are intimately connected in consciousness, and our ability to not take things personally and seriously on the path of joy is of paramount importance to the whole.

When we get caught in victim mode or stuck in suffering, it is very important to stop focusing on the little me. One way of doing this is to give yourself away. To forget yourself, give yourself. This means finding ways to help, like doing the dishes or taking the dog out for a walk. Traditionally, this has been called service. I never liked the word "service" because it always felt like work. Whenever I did find myself giving, even by accident, I was totally content because I had forgotten my BS. Of course, it took me a few years to figure that one out; I tend to be a little slow.

My tendency was to be alone whenever I had a panic attack. I was paranoid, and people plain scared me. It was as if everyone was always staring at me and judging me. The last thing I wanted to do was give, yet whenever the giving happened naturally, I would forget myself again and disappear into the path of joy.

When I was struggling with my old story of anxiety and paranoia and was taking it very personally and seriously, I felt like a total victim. I thought, "I am never going to get rid of this. Why is this happening to me?" A teacher told me the same frustrating thing I'd heard before, that everything I was going through was only to help other people. I didn't think that was very helpful to me at the time, but at least I felt less self-absorbed. It wasn't until I was in front of someone who was going through intense anxiety that I fully appreciated the truth in my teacher's words. It was like staring in a mirror.

I sense this is why most of us don't just pop without bouncing up and down for a while. We are in this pot together helping each other to pop. We help energetically because we are resting in the infinite silence but also because we can relate to each other's stories of the terrible effort we make to get free from the anxieties.

At the bottom of their hearts, we all want peace. We go through all the drama, anxiety, fear, and struggle with our stories only so we can help other people. On the path of joy, *you* are an example for humanity. This is because you are living in peace after having had to move through the process without skipping steps. Having transcended the story yourself, you can relate to those going through the same thing. This is magic.

If you were to skip all the steps and get struck with the "enlightenment beam" (like I wanted), what use would you be? You could only give blessings and hugs and stare at people and smile. By doing whatever it takes, you are a bliss warrior and protector of peace. In reaching the popcorn effect, there is tremendous power in doing the steps in the journey and not skipping them. (But of course we can't skip them, even if we try.) This is why you are a popcorn-effect superhero.

Being

The mind can mimic anything. The only thing it can't mimic is Stillness.
—Maharishi Krishnananda Ishaya, who taught me meditation and everything I don't know

Who or what am I?

If we are what we eat, I am in a lot of trouble. I might turn into candy one day. If we are what we think, then we are... yikes. I pray that we are what we are, as that would be very nice. I know it may sound simple and cheesy to say, "We are what we are," or "It is what it is." Yet this is so obvious that we tend to overlook it.

From the silence comes awareness—and content appearing within that awareness. In this awareness, we can become fascinated with the content. The content will never reveal anything new and fresh, except more changing content. Why should content be any different from what it is anyway? In the never-ending flow of changing content, our attention shifts and moves from one object to the next with no end in sight. It happens in a seamless fashion while we are thinking. The thinking includes an attraction to content that fades into disinterest. Our awareness has not been properly introduced to its source, so we perceive content as more interesting.

We become fascinated with ourselves because content is mesmerising and self-absorbing. It draws our attention like an orange Lamborghini pulling up beside us. Don't get me wrong; I love my Camry, but I usually don't catch people staring at it in the way they do a Lamborghini. Our fascination is like being in Las Vegas; before you know it, you are caught up in the shifting, bright, loud landscape. It is mesmerising and can be extremely entertaining, but also it can leave you tired, burnt out, and broke. You feel like you need a vacation after this vacation.

There is nothing wrong with fascination. Imagine you are driving, and you see a beautiful girl or guy crossing the road. It's fine to look, but if you keep your eyes on that person for more than a few seconds, you are going to get into an accident. We live our lives like accidents waiting to happen, our awareness absorbed in the show. Until something happens to break the hypnosis (like getting slapped by our partner), we keep on dreaming.

Our nature, which is pure being, is okay with or without content, yet we see ourselves more clearly once the fascination with content wears out. The content may continue, change, or vanish altogether, but whatever it does, this content has nothing to do with awakening. Again it's worth repeating: we don't have to do anything with the content in our minds. It simply is not important!

As we rest in our true nature, we are left with content but with less fascination for it. The story continues, but it loses our interest because we are more attracted to the silence. Our belief that the absorbing, story content is somehow tangible and truthful fades away and is replaced by what is. The interest is now in *big* Self-absorption of a type that is the path of joy.

It is important to understand that we don't need to *try* to become more interested in the silence versus the content. Humans are magnetically attracted to the silence. We have spent our lives resisting this natural pull. Being is infinitely more interesting, and it takes no effort at all to dive into. It only seems as if it takes effort due to the mind's habit of making an effort to achieve our desired goals. With a little familiarity with the natural enjoyment of moving inward toward the self, our efforts turn into great effortless satisfaction. Do we really need effort to eat our favourite foods or enjoy our favourite music?

Being is the source of all enjoyment, and it is delicious! This enjoyment is why traditionally we talk about the mind becoming still. It is not because we do anything to force it into stillness but because through the awe and enjoyment of stillness, everything else is abandoned. The mind actually has nothing to do with stillness. Stillness is no-mind, the Buddha Mind, or the one mind. Although the mind seems to become still through experiencing stillness, what is actually happening is that we are seeing beyond the content. In other words, mind is just another concept. Unfortunately, most of us don't know this exploration is even an option. What we have been exposed to is only a superficial part of the whole, not the fresh and alive whole itself.

At first, the stillness is easy to dismiss because it does not seem as glamorous as content. It is only what *is*, without anything special added to it. It is black coffee. It is water containing the coffee. It is space containing the water. It is nothingness containing the space. What *is* doesn't move while the content appears to move. Stillness is nothing and everything. What we search for ultimately is projected in our mind's eye as some form to be attained. (The mind could also be considered form or content.) Who or what is looking for this form? The tricky thing is, the content can even appear as formless content— a thought of stillness.

As we become more conscious, the content in our awareness becomes more slippery and subtle and perhaps spiritual in flavour. What is sometimes not so clear to us spiritual people (I am sorry for labelling us) is that a spiritual object in the mind is a fantastic form or content appearing and nothing more or less valuable than anything else that appears in consciousness. We already are nothingness (black coffee), and the special spiritual ideas or idols (cream and sugar) we chase are a lovely play of consciousness. There is only nothingness (silence) playing, yet in the playing appears everything, including the search for being. This search turns the formless being into content—an object of form. Then we chase our tail, going in circles.

Being is a wonderful mystery hiding in plain sight. This reminds me of the quote, "If you see the Buddha, kill the

Buddha." In other words, the content of Buddha is obviously not the ultimate concept-free Buddha we already are. The pure mind is the Buddha mind, which is *no* mind. Go ahead and see if you can find the mind. I have never found it.

This is why the Buddha said, "I truly attained nothing from complete, unexcelled Enlightenment." The Buddha cannot find Buddha because the Buddha is already Buddha. This discovery is enlightenment for "no one." Upon awakening, the individual does not receive a special Buddha enlightenment kit with a Buddha hat and cane (as a bonus for sitting in the sun for weeks and for not being able to feel your legs anymore).

I used to be an impure soul once. To rationalise not drinking my coffee black as my teacher did, I told him that the cream and sugar were bliss and joy. He said, "Look, just try it black for two weeks, and you will never go back." I agreed to it. At first it was like drinking nothing, boring with no flavour at all. Then after a week, I started to taste the depth and subtleties of the bean. (This works only with freshly ground beans.) After two weeks of black coffee, I woke up with a desire to put cream and sugar back in my coffee again out of habit. As I was walking to work, I took a sip, spat it out, bent over, and almost threw up on the side of the road. Wow, he was right—he is indeed a coffee wizard or bean whisperer.

If we have been lucky enough to taste the stillness, it can enliven a magnetism or drawing power within us. It is an attractive power, so attractive that millions of people have dedicated their lives to searching for it. Even though we are often misled by ideas of truth or the desire to attain something outside ourselves, the stillness remains, underlying all the ideas and desires and the searching itself. The apparent twists and turns on the path are also the beautiful dance of nothings (being) looking to be somethings (content).

Finally, we rest in contentment as beings that enjoy themselves while content flows by unobstructed. Being alive is a spontaneous adventure, and in this aliveness, even the most ordinary events are miracles happening out of nowhere.

Allowing

Every experience comes so we can know God more.
—Maharishi Krishnananda Ishaya

In life, everything comes to us exactly so that we can keep choosing to move toward freedom, and "what we resist persists." Have you noticed the same pattern happening over and over again? Even if we see the pattern and are trying to let it go, it just keeps popping up, especially if it is one we badly want to be rid of. Underlying those patterns is a thought such as, "If I could only get rid of this, I would be free or have more peace!" Is there anything we can do to speed up that process?

Some of us comfortably assume, "Well, that's life," and don't bother to do anything except complain and gossip like victims (either in our minds or out loud). Others are willing to try anything to be free of annoying habits and addictions. I have alternated between the two, at times feeling like a victim and then getting inspired to free myself from identifying with the mind. (Looking back, it is funny how many strange things I tried, but I guess that is part of the game.) These obstacles prevent us from moving forward, and nothing seems to make particular thoughts disappear permanently.

These thoughts are plain old sticky ones that beg us to pay attention to them because of our habit of not being aware. Instead of interest in silence, we put importance and energy into their specialness. This is like falling asleep at the wheel; then we crash only to keep repeating the same pattern over and over again. They seem more real than ordinary thoughts since we feel them in our guts. They may even make us want to throw up. We are doing nothing wrong; the attention consciousness has given them has nothing to do with you. You have no control over what thoughts come up—only over your relationship to them. All we can do is be more aware; this is how we get the momentum of allowing moving into full swing. How can we allow the underlying patterns when we are not even aware. Don't be afraid to look; I promise you won't die. In fact you might even start to enjoy it like a game of hide and seek.

When we are in charge of running our own "enlightenment show," it becomes about escaping from *this* to be free from *that*. How can we be free if we're not free from *it* (whatever it may be)? Yet escaping from experiences is not the answer to freedom. By trying to be free *from* our experiences, we interrupt the natural flow of love that allows us to be free *to* experience. The problem is not the experience on its own; the problem is "me" and my identification with the experience. By focusing attention on the pattern and on what I can do to escape it, I keep it in place by resisting it. By focusing attention on the source of what allows it, I experience anything without any problem. This is freedom— attention on what does not change yet allows change to happen is what manifests contentment.

Can you imagine what it would be like to allow your experiences without trying to change them? If it seems difficult, it is only because you feel as if you need to do something with your experiences. That's okay! Why not allow that feeling and see what happens? You may not be free according to your idea of freedom, but you can certainly pretend to be free or to act as if you are. Freedom starts with allowing. Remember what Manyu says: "Just Pretend."

Allowing all that is, including all identification, loosens us from the grip of tension. The separate individual cannot allow, but we can allow it to function as it is designed to. This functioning is just a natural part of a puppet show. We can even allow energetic tension as it is happening. The puppet has no control over what happens to it. Our essential nature is what allows the puppet to function, not the puppet itself.

By exploring the natural way of being in the silence, we can start to play like the silence plays. By playing like spirit plays, we become spirit. What we play like, we are. If we play as a separate individual trying to achieve and acquire, that's what we become. If we play like the infinite that allows and never takes the play seriously, we will see how our infinite nature is playing.

The truth is, we can't stop the flow of experiences heading toward us. If we knew that they were designed for our awakening, we wouldn't want to stop them. When we look back at them from a place of clarity, we can see these experiences as necessary steps. When we see the beauty and perfection of our life as it has unfolded into truth, we find it easier to accept what comes next. Every weird and strange step (that's me labelling the nature of my steps) is needed; otherwise it would never have appeared in the first place.

I think it was Jesus who said, "I go before you to prepare a place for you." To me this says, "Just keep walking; every step of the way I am there with you." Experience is the next step on your journey. You don't need to know what form it will take because that is the surprise. For heaven's sake, do not take it personally; it is just another step to allow you to keep walking. But if you happen to take it personally, allow yourself to. Who knows, maybe that is the last step. Everything and every step will prepare you to know God more and therefore to "know thyself."

Everything appears out of a still field of nothingness that is much like a movie screen. The screen has no opinion about all the images that appear. Being or stillness also has no opinions about what moves through it; it simply allows everything to appear. The separate individual is the one who wants to change what is happening. But what are we? Are we the stillness of being or the character who appears out of the nothingness? Let's explore that and find out for ourselves what we are.

It would be nice to exchange the movements in our heads and bodies for another's. Buddha's movements ("I want to get up, but I can't feel my legs") might be sweeter than ours. But even if we changed ours for those of the next-door neighbours, we probably wouldn't take them so seriously— maybe we would even laugh at them. My teacher said during a retreat, "Imagine if you could unscrew your head and put somebody else's on." That would be funny. What the other person took personally would make us laugh. Even if the thoughts were similar to ours, they would not be ours. No thoughts are personal; they just appear in being. Being is not taking them personally because it is bigger than that. You are bigger than the thoughts because you are being.

At the very core of our being is allowing. We can observe where all movement comes from, such as thoughts and feelings and actions. In order to have movement, you have to have

stillness, and movement must be allowed to come from stillness; otherwise it would not have appeared. The stillness appears to move like the sound of silence sounding.

Everything about you—your story, and your past, present, and future—is always allowed. Since you are allowed to appear on this screen (even as you identify yourself as a separate person), why wouldn't you allow yourself to be okay with everything happening? The good, the bad, and the ugly are all a function of appearances. Why fight it? Ultimately, it's as easy as being you or allowing yourself to be. Until you can totally allow everything in the universe as it is, keep playing with allowing.

Compassion

Before we can experience or even understand true compassion, we must be compassionate to ourselves. When we can do this, then we can heal humanity. Let's begin with *ahimsa*. *Ahimsa* is a Sanskrit word that means non-violence. We believe superficially that non-violence means not hurting others physically, mentally, or emotionally. Yet it is impossible to be non-violent unless *ahimsa* is the foundation to our being. We are all connected, and our way of thinking affects us individually and collectively. That we are connected is a blessing because it makes it ridiculously easy to heal the world by focusing on ourselves first. The world sees this as selfish, but focusing on ourselves is a selfless act that is the only way to make a lasting positive effect on the whole. If we don't heal ourselves first, we will continue to pollute our environment by energetically projecting violence into the world. This is how powerful we are.

Through non-violence, we enliven the popcorn effect by resonating with the perfection of all humanity that is underneath the appearance of suffering.

Non-violence is something that can be practised like a technique as suggested in ancient traditions. As well, *ahimsa* describes our natural way of being. *Ahimsa* is already present in the silence before awakening, during awakening, and in unity. To the extent that we are less violent with ourselves, we can see through to this true nature and into the heart of everything in the universe. This gentleness moves into the world offering peace. This peace is a true solution.

The exploration of silence reveals the non-violent power of the stillness, which instantly removes any chance of getting hurt or hurting others. The ultimate invincibility of *ahimsa* is so powerful that it needs no protection. When there is no self-violence, only the untouched innocence of the divine remains.

The first step is to see that we are being violent with ourselves and begin to move toward gentleness. Violence comes from the habit of unconsciously accepting thoughts as real. We believe in these self-destructive thoughts and pay for this belief by maintaining old patterns of suffering. But we don't need to keep reinforcing the old limiting structures we have built. There is no rule that says we have to believe in our thoughts. Where did we pick them up in the first place? Consciousness has innocently picked them up.

Once we start the awareness engine, we can begin to see through the false structures that are pulling the strings on our puppets. Like an alcoholic who is powerless to stop drinking, we have become powerless to stop beating ourselves up. This strange addiction keeps us locked into victim mode. We feel or have been told that we have unconscious habits we need to discover, but what can we do with the unconscious? By being aware of the silence, we become more familiar or conscious of all our habits. At first we can be shocked to see just how hard we are on ourselves. With practice we start taking these thoughts less seriously until finally we are laughing at them.

The infinite is not violent and makes no judgments; it is only our own conditioning that keeps this violent cycle going. Our brains have been wired a certain way, but the good news is that we can restore them to their original state of innocence. Sure, we can't do anything about what is unconscious, but the more we practise awareness of what is conscious, the more the unconscious aspects comes into the light. Once we see that we have given a thought reality, it loses power. The next time the same thought comes, it will be easier to allow it and let it go without believing in its reality. This is the dawn of true compassion, where violence cannot survive the gentleness of love and wisdom.

Even practising being gentle can be a frustrating task in the beginning. "I am trying to be gentle, but it's not working! I will never get this!" These violent thought that goes on unnoticed.

Ahimsa is already effortlessly within what you are. You don't have to manufacture it. Being aware of what is going on is enough; this brings it into the light, and as a result, it begins to lose its attractiveness. A noticed thought is already non-violent, even if its content is violent, because it has lost its power in the light of being witnessed. By practising, we get better at noticing.

Thoughts only seem to have power because they are allowed to go on unnoticed. Without our awareness, they act unconsciously as a puppet master pulling the strings to create a false reality. These thoughts become our adopted truth or our way of perceiving the world. This is the hypnosis of what we think we are. It may be suggested that you are unworthy of peace or that you will never get what you want. Now count to ten and open your eyes.

Exploring the silence magnifies the natural ability to be aware of the non-violence already present. The "oh shit" moments (when we judge ourselves for not being good enough) become the "oh sweet—I am aware" moments when our attitude shifts to gratitude for the miracle of being aware. Please be kind and gentle to your awareness, as it can't help being aware.

Ahimsa is most powerful in the purity of silence. Even if thoughts and feelings seem to disturb that harmless reality, it's only because of a habit. Playing with being gentle and aware develops a new, more positive habit. There is no rule that says you have to believe in your past thoughts; your job is to be gentler with yourself and take your thoughts less seriously. You could see them as quacking ducks. Ahimsa sees violence as a crazy-looking, wild, dancing duck, an image that looks a little silly.

Now that we are gentler, we can be compassionate toward ourselves and others. This gives us space, allowing what we experience on the path of joy. This compassion overflows into humanity as we finally have the capacity to hold someone in the light of what they are. They are no longer victims of circumstance; they are the same shining divinity we are.

The waking up of compassion can be fuel for our commitment to God when we see it's not about *me* and *my* path. Seeing this makes it easier to let go of our special stuff we tightly hold onto. It's inspiring to know that when we let go of this stuff, it is easier for all of us to let go since we are in the same pool. When you pee in the pool, it affects us all. The idea that we are in this pool together certainly helped me a lot when I was trying to let go of my anxiety. I thought that if it was true that letting it go would lighten the load of all the other anxious people suffering, then I would do it. I would do it for them, not for "little me."

After all, they say there is this mass consciousness and that we are connected in this field. A lot of us add junk to the field constantly through thought, anxiety, fears, etc. But when we add peace and non-violence to that field through our inner choice, the magic starts to happen. Gentleness, non-violence, and compassion are immensely more powerful than self-absorbed thinking. They send ripples out into the field, inviting expansion rather than contraction.

When we wake up, we wake up for everyone because it is the same divinity. This represents the true meaning of the Bodhisattva, or wisdom being, where we become the Buddha. Within this divinity is an infinite compassion, a powerful ocean of love and wisdom that divinely fuels everything into full Buddhahood.

One of the meanings of the Bodhisattva vow in Buddhism is that we should wait to attain full liberation after all souls have been liberated. This idea sounds very noble and appeals to our willingness to help humanity. The logic behind this is flawed, however. Buddha didn't wait, so why should you? The idea that holding back your bliss or liberation is somehow useful, noble, or compassionate is a joke. This would be like a kernel of popcorn choosing not to pop for the sake of all the kernels. All that happens is that one more kernel is stuck in the pot. This kernel gets harder and crustier and will never pop.

We don't help our brothers and sisters by suffering and identifying with limitations. This seems obvious, yet compassion is mistaken for empathy in the modern world. The best thing to do is live by example and hold out your hand.

Exploring the silence becomes invaluable because the wisdom of compassion invites another to the same playing field, one without suffering. The wisdom of compassion sees divine perfection in another and holds them to that. This is an energetic happening and not necessarily about what is done or said. The self that is resting in the infinite sees the same infinite in others regardless of appearances. This, more than anything, creates the magical popcorn effect, allowing for compassion to perform miracles in people's lives.

Compassion is the fuel that dissolves all obstacles, even when those obstacles are so subtle they can't be seen. This Buddha fuel allows us to burn through "to infinity and beyond." How we awaken can determine whether we pop in seconds or years. The compassion of all the enlightened sages before us, silently cheering us on, gives us that extra Buddha boost to stay on the razor's edge.

As we move along the path, we can get stuck in ugly experiences that become immediately obvious from the intense contrast between them and the inner peace we experience. We can move through these experiences almost instantly when we have mastered *ahimsa* and compassion. However, we may develop a new problem that some puppets might even be jealous of—a beautiful kind of being stuck can now occur as we cruise along in our self-exploration.

We can get stuck in or plateau in a semi-joyful experience; we can't see that it's just another lovely place along our infinite journey. For obvious reasons, many people get caught in these lovely places. It feels great to have peace and joy in contrast to the pain of the past. Who can blame someone who wants to set up camp in that forest of peace? Silence is infinite, however, and the path of joy is a compassionate friend reminding us to let go of that lovely experience as well. That which is real can never be lost. Holding on to an experience that comes and goes because of our fear of loss means denying what is available to us now. This is the grace of God desiring to give us the whole pie, not just a piece of it.

Nothing is so special that it can't be let go of. Only by letting everything go can we enter the aliveness of being. As we dissolve in the silence, we are being pulled along an infinite expansion of consciousness and do not have to get stuck at any particular point in the infinite. Though it is nice to be stuck in awe at the door to Heaven, let's not forget that it is just the doorway. You can stop drooling and keep walking further into Heaven.

The quickest way to let go of something is to not pick it up in the first place—even Baby Jesus knew that!

Staying in the silence now is an effect of compassion that happens in unity. This is the most powerful effect of all, as well as the simplest. Staying in the silence now is the most compassionate thing a human being can do because it is the most selfless of acts. It is so selfless that there is no one there being compassionate—there exists only infinite compassion as it is.

Nothing is in the way of that.

Heart

The indescribable Heart is the mirror in which all (i.e., the entire universe) appears.
The one single consciousness, the space of mere being, alone is the primal and supreme thing, the silent whole.
—Sri Muruganar
(Sri Muruganar is a poet and student of Ramana Maharishi, who composed sayings from Ramana's talks. Each saying was checked by Ramana Maharishi himself.)

As large as the universe outside, even so large is the universe within the Lotus of the Heart.
Within it are Heaven and Earth, the Sun, the Moon, the lightening, and all the stars.
—Chandogya Upanishad (8:1:3)

How big is a heart?

The heart is one of the most amazing mysteries. The beauty of the heart is indescribable. Its presence is felt in the silence, at the core of everything wonderful. It is seen in poetry, music, art, crystals, plants, human beings, cosmic beings. An independent survey suggests that 93 per cent of all extraterrestrials have hearts too. The other 7 per cent are covered with goo.

Many in this world are very familiar with having a broken heart or a heart that feels separate from the whole. Often it is hard to even discern what we feel separate from. Looking back now, I could describe it as feeling separate from God (silence). I felt this separation at a very young age, and it seemed to follow me throughout my childhood and into adulthood. Even being spiritual seemed to make the pain of separation worse. The empty hole I felt in my heart was a huge motivator to seek God; yet at the same time, the more seeking I did, the more intense was the sense of separation. I was always on the lookout for anything that would seem to fill the hole, but it was always a temporary fix. My favourite hole-filler was the chiller from Second Cup; later I evolved to the Starbuck's Frappuccino and then finally to the more advanced black coffee.

Most people go through being disheartened. The desire to want to fix this and fill the hole is natural. As we ascend from being disheartened by falling in love with the silence, we begin to lose the learned, false ideas surrounding the heart. The heart reveals its absolute innocence almost as if by magic. One day we wake up and can feel it all—the pain and the joy—and yet somehow the heart is magically at peace with it all. The heart's invincibility unmasks the dualities of the inner world by robbing them of their illusory power.

As a child, I remember shutting down my emotions because I was taught that certain ways of expressing them were unacceptable. As a result, I repressed certain aspects of myself and locked them away in the dark. In psychology, they call this hidden side the shadow. I spent my energy trying to control my emotions so I could fit into the many different situations life brought. I started to act as if I had multiple personality disorder, acting differently with different people and in different situations to receive love, attention, and approval. Never was it acceptable to just be me—nor did I even have a clue what being me meant.

Later I desired to be free from my emotions, or at least free to express them. This conflicted with my strong desire to control them as they were surfacing. The constant struggle between the two desires—expressing versus suppressing—was frustrating. I was terrified that if I released my emotions I would go crazy or perhaps hurt someone.

After some time playing with the silence, my heart, which I had tried to keep secret from myself and the world for so long, started to open. I started to feel a genuine love, but at the same time, old feelings emerged; I never would have allowed them to see the light of day before. This emergence was a scary and magical event because I saw that to have no control is the true freedom of the heart. I allowed my emotions to harmlessly come to light, thereby allowing even more love to flow.

As we touch the infinite space of love, everything is free to flow. The path of joy suddenly bursts open for a moment to clear a space for us to breathe. To some this might look like a volcanic eruption, while to others it might appear a gentle breeze. By allowing it to move, you are freeing up more energy to keep exploring the movement of unmoving eternal love. This is the mystery of the heart.

The heart knows, while I know nothing. What is your *heart's greatest desire*? Follow the heart. Where does it take you?

What you choose to put your heart into grows, yet you cannot choose what the heart *is* in essence. That ability is beyond our control. Whether it's pure or impure, the heart exists in immaculate perfection, shining as a clear mirror of life. It is never satisfied until that mirror does not pretend to be a separate broken mirror. The heart only appears separate through identification with the objects reflected. This phenomenon apparently scatters attention into "bad" and "good" reflections, but in truth, the heart reflects everything innocently without judgment or control.

Every emotion comes to us only so that we can learn to freely love ourselves no matter what. Through non-violence and allowing, we turn into masters of emotion. We are masters not because we can stop and redirect emotion as if we were pulling the strings but because we know the invincibility of our heart's true nature.

It is said that "love casts out fear." In this invincibility, in which we allow all emotion without manipulation, a natural equilibrium develops over time as the heart settles in its rightful throne of silence. Finally, when we no longer care what arises within the body, and not a moment sooner, we feel joy, peace, and love. The love merges in the silence as one, and all else is quiet in the inner sea.

Innocence

Master Innocence and you master Consciousness.
—Maharishi Krishnananda Ishaya

Innocence is invincible and indestructible.

In innocence we enter this world, absorbing all the beliefs and programmes we can get our little hands on (consciously and unconsciously). Innocence has no reason to distrust; it accepts everything as it is. Seemingly, we need to protect our innocence from the world to feel safe. But when we experience its nature, we are free from the world and therefore free from the need to protect it.

The innocence of what we are remains always untouched and gets clearer as we practice letting go and staying open. By consciously remembering the original innocence of our nature, we see through our programming and adopted beliefs. It is not that all programming and conditioning disappear; this would make it difficult to remember how to tie our shoelaces. But the self-destructive programming keeping us separate no longer serves a master of innocence.

We are now waking up out of auto-puppet mode. Wake up and smell the coffee (or hear the popcorn popping). What is there to feel guilty about? When we allow the power of an innocence that loves, accepts, and plays to move within our being, magic happens in our life. That same power that innocently accepted the false now sees through it into the reality of the path of joy.

When we were children, magic was our natural playground. It was only a dream that we lost the innocence and somehow did something wrong; nothing actually happened. The attention of our consciousness moved into a belief in a separate puppet, but consciousness only appeared to move.

Our nervous systems and brains make us act like puppets from the programming they have received. It is interesting to view our lives at a distance to see how little control we have over our own decisions and actions. Usually automatic reactions occur before we even realise what is happening. Our world can consist of unconscious movement from our programming, as if we are sleepwalking. Of course, we assume we are the ones in charge and responsible for our actions, but is that the whole truth?

By exploring the silence and allowing, we confirm by experience that our innocence is indeed intact and unaffected by the conditioning of the mind or the actions of the puppet. We innocently believed whatever was introduced into the mind. It then became our reality, our truth, and what we know about ourselves (which is always what we *think* we know about ourselves).

I suspect that the innocence we came from before we were born had no reason to doubt. Why would this eternal innocence doubt or question anything? Only now in our maturity do we see a reason to question the positions and beliefs we adopted. These old habits are no longer useful and at worst extremely harmful to us and the rest of humanity.

All it takes is one person playing in innocence for it to catch on. If you don't know how, just start and pretend you do. Playing with innocence is magic.

By continuing to discover what the silence is and how to relax into it, the innocence automatically starts bubbling up even despite not knowing how to be innocent. Before you know it, you are on a path of joy and playing like a little kid. One minute you bump your head on the table (you take something serious) and the next moment you are jumping on the couch. It does not matter what age you are; some adults are even more innocent than children.

Innocence is not about how you act but how you approach life as it comes. Will you let the next moment come without knowing exactly what it should look like? Will you get frustrated when it doesn't meet expectations? Innocence allows what comes to come, no matter what the mind says good, bad, right or wrong. The Silence is pure innocence; discover that and the whole playground is yours.

Love

When you Love yourself completely you will be Free.
—Maharishi Krishnanada Ishaya

What conquers all? What moves mountains? It is *love, love, love.*
Love is magic. Real love dissolves everything into itself. Where
there is love, there is freedom.

Imagine what would happen if you loved yourself
completely—enough to accept what you don't like about your
character. True freedom isn't just transcending limitations. True
freedom accepts the limitations of being human because there is
no one left to identify with these limits. Love transforms the
limitation into perfection—not by making it disappear, but by
loving it. Love embraces and accepts the humanness, making it
divine to be human.

What does a sage look like to you? There is a misconception
about this (not that he looks like anything at all). I saw the image
of a bald Asian man with a white goatee dressed in red robes. His
experience was beyond anything I could imagine, and he was
mysterious, had magical powers, and was transcendent, having
no thoughts or emotions. He only experienced divine bliss, and
he only spoke wise words. Perfectly beyond human, he had
transcended his humanity. He didn't talk very much, just sat
levitating in the lotus posture with a blissful, radiant smile on his
face.

When I met teachers of truth, I would often compare them to
the image I had in my head and then determine whether they
were enlightened or not. The problem was that I was always
comparing myself to this sage image as well. This freedom I
wanted was kept at a distance, in a galaxy far, far away, since I
was chasing a fantasy ideal. This sage image is very popular with
seekers, and we all have one as long as we see ourselves as
separate.

When I started to explore the silence in meditation, I noticed that my idea of freedom started to change and evolve along with my own experience. Reading different books, exploring teachings, and seeing different teachers opened up my mind a little. Maybe I didn't know as much as I'd thought.

Even though my idea of freedom was expanding, the pain of comparing myself to those around me, who I assumed were "there," was becoming even more intense. Only one thing was certain to me: they had something I was missing. I struggled to dissolve those parts of me that were clearly in the way of my ideal goal. "When I can get rid of these emotions and thoughts, I will be free," I thought. "When I stop my mind, I will be free. I have to practise my look of stillness so that they can see what I have. It's all in the eyes."

One day I got totally fed up with myself and all this effort, so I decided to just give up trying to reach my idea of freedom. I made a deal with myself: for two weeks I would be okay with everything happening in my mind, good or bad. I just trusted that the universe was not stupid and knew what I wanted. If enlightenment happened, fine, but I was done trying to get it. Basically, I hit the reset button and started again with these new rules.

When I was comparing, I was okay with the act of comparing. When I was judging myself, I did not judge myself for judging. Very quickly I started to notice that I had stopped being so obsessed with freedom. In fact, all my ideas of freedom went out the window. I felt like a newborn, as if I knew absolutely nothing. However, I became even more committed to my meditation practice. Surrendering became more effortless and natural, short-ening the times I was in auto-puppet mode.

Suddenly, everything happening in life was absolutely okay, and the silence became infinitely loving of everything going on. This was both an inner and outer acceptance of what was happening. Out of this came a deep acceptance of myself that turned into an incredible and simple love. I remember being aware of my latest concept of freedom as it came up: *freedom is to love myself*. I thought, "Wow, you are loving yourself for the first time." I even loved my puppet (puppet love). It felt great to be okay with everything.

Later on, I had the insight that because there is only unchanging silence, anything that was changing in my mind, such as my ideas of freedom, couldn't be real. My idea that freedom was to love myself was not the same as being empty *for the love*. The wisdom of knowing nothing was the path of joy and the coming home to infinite love.

Have you ever felt as if you were just faking, as in, "Fake it until you make it?" If you do not know anything or hold any more concepts about enlightenment, what else can you do? How will your puppet interact in the world? Just fake it and see what happens.

The stillness is what it is and does what it does, but what can we do about it? A teacher once compared life to a video game. When we go to work, we enter a video game. Some of the games have more levels than others. In an apprentice game, there are four levels, and at each level you have to complete everything to get to the next level. Sometimes an apprentice can stop having fun and get stuck in the game. We get stuck in it when we take it seriously. Life is full of these levels, and just like a video game we get rewarded for our achievements as we complete them. Our avatars get more or less status in the game. What if we let go of our avatars? Would the game disappear?

Sometimes the rewards we receive are material, and other times they are a sense of achievement. What everyone in the world wants is to be loved. This is the motivation behind all movement in the world. It seems distorted, but if you innocently explore the root of choices, you will find the desire to be loved.

Freedom and love, however, do not work like this; you will never *achieve* them. They are impossible to acquire or to lose. The only thing that can happen is that one game ends and another begins. In the movie *War Games*, the computer realises that the only way to win the game is to not play at all. This is the end game of the ego and the beginning of the play of divine love. In this game, we pretend that we are taking the games of the world seriously, but in truth we are just pretending. We are treading lightly on the world—in it but not of it.

Laughter yoga is a good example of the power of pretending. In a room of people fake laughing, we start laughing for real, even though we don't feel like it. (The mind says it's ridiculous.) This is another example of the popcorn effect. The reverse happens when you go into a room full of people taking themselves and the world seriously; this is called the burnt or soggy popcorn effect.

Being is the ultimate pretender, acting as a separate character in the game yet always absolutely free from the game. Liberation takes the separation out of the character so there is only a joyful expression of playing. We are always pretending and acting. Love is embracing this game of life and all its levels, allowing us to play without *any* restrictions.

Some of us believe that we are unlovable and unworthy, which seems very real. We label and define where we think we are in the game of freedom. This artificial boundary limits the amount of love we can receive from the world at any one moment. But it doesn't matter where we are in the game because we are only pretending to be in it—this is the cosmic joke. We love pretending to climb the ladder when there is no actual ladder. Instead of pretending to be unworthy of love, why not pretend that you love everything about you?

When you love yourself totally, you move from unconscious pretending to the freedom to witness all pretending emerging from love. Then the fun begins. Freedom is loving yourself enough to just be yourself—*all of yourself.*

Path of the Sages

What follows is the story of how the path of the sages found me.

On one of my retreats, the teacher talked about two basic paths that humanity is on. One is called the path of the gods, and the other the path of the sages. Virtually everyone is on the path of the gods, a long road designed to satisfy desire after desire until finally (after a million lives), the highest desire is for the truth, which results in waking up. The path of the sages, however, is the joyful, swift path in which exploring the truth as the highest desire occurs now. This path does not waste any time and is out of time altogether. It's a path that throws the process away and says, "This is it, now. Take a deep breath and dive."

I tend to think of myself as a bit of an expert on the path of the gods. After all, I had been walking down that winding road for quite some time. Actually, I think we all are experts to some degree.

I had a large meditation room in my house. It was a humble room designed to actualise my personal ascension/enlightenment. I had pictures of ascended masters, angels, and ancient, alien symbols placed strategically on the walls. I would stare at them to feel the unique energy pouring out of the pictures and symbols. On the floor, I had placed a queen-sized wool blanket to absorb all the good energy coming down from above and up from below. In the centre was my regular cushion (with no special powers, I am ashamed to say). My altar was comprised of a huge poster of a guru from India, incense, and a big Tibetan bowl filled with every crystal I could get my hands on. My walls were filled with hundreds of my books, spaced between the larger crystals in the corners and centres of the walls. From the ceiling hung hundreds of small crystals; a larger one hung over my crown chakra to give me that extra boost I needed to get to God. I would sit on my cushion with my most powerful crystal of the day, reading my books and contemplating the truth. I was filling my mind with the most wonderful ideas to beat everyone in the race to enlightenment.

One sunny summer day, my Aunt Suzie came over to get a tour of the house after my girlfriend and I had settled in. We were chatting as we walked around, taking a look at each room. Then she opened the door to my sacred room, walked in, paused, gasped, and ran out. I was insulted and thought, "Oh she probably can't handle the high vibrational energy." God knows what kind of alien energies I had been invoking in the room that week.

At least what I was involved in was entertaining and kept me busy moving into the light. I had downloaded 71 per cent of total planetary light. I was also working with Archangel Metatron to get some of that cosmic light as well. Working with the angels was fun, but my heart wanted more.

Energetically, I was out of my body most of the time. A healer friend had to remind me that I had lower chakras as well as higher ones. I spent most of my time in my crown chakra trying to fly out into the cosmos. Dealing with the world and the mundane things it brought with it was not on my to-do list.

I had been enlightened many times before (or so I thought). The last time was when I created a circle of quartz crystals, sat in it, and announced to God and the universe, "This is it—I am going to get enlightened now." So I put on the *om* music and started to rub my biggest crystal from India all over my chest, head, and arms to get that light and wisdom inside me.

Even during those days while contemplating what I thought was the truth, I would sometimes by accident slip into this peaceful silence and would wonder with a sense of wishing, "What if it were this simple? What if the truth has something to do with surrendering into this silence, this still presence? Nah! It could not be that easy—otherwise everyone would get it," I told myself.

Soon after, while at home reading a huge book about infinity, my mind started to expand intensely with a huge concept of the way reality works. At the same time, the pain contracted my heart equally, and I could no longer take it. I broke down and cried out, "If there is a God, please help me. I am done with all this effort." Silence and peace filled my mind, and I experienced the relief of oneness for an instant, enough to let go of my obsession with the race.

Two months later, I was at work flipping through the newspaper, and an ad for a cheesy psychic fair in town caught my eye. I had wanted to go and find out who I was in a past life. I wanted to know the reason why I was so messed up. Why was I so desperate to find the truth? Why couldn't I be normal like other people and just live my life? I felt that maybe I had been a Tibetan monk because I was so passionate to discover truth. Then again, I could have been someone bad who needed to do good deeds (like heal the world) to balance their karma. For whatever reason, I felt compelled to go find out about my past lives, so I went to the fair.

When I arrived that evening, I found the booth where they were giving past-life readings, and I waited. I somehow knew that I had found the person I needed to talk to. I waited for about half an hour for her to show up. While sitting across from me, she began to get choked up, tears in her eyes. She told me how difficult this was going to be. I thought, "Holy shit, who the heck was I? I guess I can cross Tibetan monk off the list." She then proceeded to tell me I was the worst person imaginable. Instead of being upset, I felt surprisingly wonderful because it gave me some reason for all these feelings I had growing up.

After about half an hour of listening to the psychic, I was getting a little bored. "Okay, I get it. I was bad, but what am I going to do about it?" I asked. She said not to worry—these lives were not linear, and I'd had other lives, but this one was the most interesting. I said to her, "I practise this thing called ascension and—"

Very boldly she cut me off and said, "That is not the true ascension! True ascension is here in the form of The Bright Path; Christ is here!"

I thought, "Wow, I've finally met someone as strange as me." Yet something about her passion convinced me to really listen.

She told me how The Bright Path meditation had changed her life, and that even though all day she was talking about past and future lives, she has never been so "in the now." We had a good laugh at that irony. She then handed me some material about The Bright Path, and I sat reading articles about enlightenment being simple, easy, and natural. It sounded too good to be true, but it was exactly what I was searching for. I had to find out more. But before I did that, I went to the best and most famous past-life readers I could find to confirm what she had said because I couldn't let that go so easily. I also talked to a swami and a spiritual teacher and got their opinions. Eventually, I calmed down and began to focus on what I wanted instead of wondering about why I was the way I was.

A swami explained my need to ask why. He said that at the psychological level, we are so desperate for meaning that if our story in this life doesn't explain why we are as we are, we will look elsewhere. He said people who are sensitive at this level of the mind can find a story that will satisfy this need. Whether or not this has anything to do with past lives is not the point. The relief comes because we have an understanding. I understood why I felt so condemned, for example. Being inquisitive (obsessed with past lives), I started to get readings from all the best readers I could find. Some took me into hypnosis, and others just shared their information.

I would describe my pain to each reader and ask if there was a reason for it. Each one gave me the most fascinating story to explain it, all with incredible detail. I literally wanted to go get popcorn because this was way better than a movie; it was my movie, about me! Sometimes the stories conflicted in the timeline, like when I was a Japanese Kamikaze *and* a Nazi during World War II. Who knows, maybe I was both. After all, we are beyond space and multi-dimensional in nature, aren't we?

It was funny that the universe used my insane curiosity about past lives to hand me the greatest gift, one that would open my heart to the path of joy. Yet I would continue to spend more time looking into the past. That's the pull of the path of the gods—we do whatever we can do to keep the story going in the past or future.

At the time I was so open to anything that would work, I was ready to go anywhere in the world. I had to find out who taught this meditation I had heard about at the psychic fair. After a long, hard search, I was very happy to discover this group was in Vancouver. At the time, I was living in Calgary, Alberta. I thought, "Wow, how lucky am I that they're so close." In February 1999, I booked my flight for Vancouver.

I remember entering the house where the group met and asking this guy who was dressed in black and relaxing on the couch, "Does this stuff actually work?" I will never forget his smile. I knew this was for real.

I tried to keep both the concepts and the peace at the same time; however, the silence came to be much more delicious than holding onto what I had struggled to achieve. Eventually, it all collapsed, and I realised my struggle to climb the ladder had all been a cosmic Joke. They say, "The intellect is a ladder too short." Thank God my intellect was short in the first place, so it didn't take too long to reach full capacity. Like some people, I tended to exaggerate the size of my ladder to boost my self-esteem.

The path of the gods is like a ladder with levels and initiations that continue until we reach God or the infinite. Most of us don't even recognise God as the target, but this is normal until we start longing for something more out of life. This could take lifetimes. This is why in the *Bhagavad Gita* it says, "Out of a thousand, one will long for me, out of a thousand who long for me; one will seek me, and out of a thousand who seek me, one will know me in Truth." We are very lucky to even have the desire to know what we are. It is rare. Finding God is the rarest of treasures, especially on the path of the gods.

There are many different forms this path may take. Always the goal is outside our reach and will happen sometime in the future but never now. There is nothing wrong with this, and I honour and respect that path for what it is. But this path that keeps the peace of God in the future is just not as fun for me anymore. The good news is that this path is only an option and not necessary for all of us.

The path of the sages is synonymous with the path of joy. Indeed, joy is the quickest path because it is in alignment with the reality of what is now. There is nothing wrong with the path of the gods, but if you want enlightenment at popcorn speed, make it the path of the sages.

Staying on the Razor's Edge

Devotion

> Not forgetting consciousness (i.e., not forgetting one's own Self-consciousness due to pramada or inattentiveness) is the path of devotion (bhakti), the relationship of unfading real love, because the real consciousness of Self, which shines as the undivided (non-dual) supreme bliss itself, surges as the nature of love (or bhakti).
> Sri Muruganar

I think we want proof ahead of time that commitment to our highest desires will bring actual results. If you have ever wanted anything really badly and achieved it, you know commitment works. This commitment can seem like effort in the beginning, but once it is set in motion it becomes effortless. After all, do you really have to work hard to give your attention to what brings you joy? The path of joy is always easier to commit to because it is the most enjoyable practice in the world. It is a joy that makes chocolate taste better and green beans not as bad as they usually do.

A little commitment goes a long way. Commitment transforms into effortless devotion to continue doing what brings us happiness. As we continue along the path of joy, we get more clarity about what we are doing in life, and this gives us space to be truly content with what life brings to us naturally.

Anthony de Mello said, "Enlightenment is: absolute cooperation with the inevitable." No matter what arises on our path, devotion will see us through it. We can allow everything because our eye is focused on Heaven.

Clarity is a wonderful thing to have, but sometimes we need to cooperate with the inevitable confusion that arises on our spiritual journey. When we have clarity, life becomes simple and obvious. But when life doesn't go as expected, we can get confused about where we are going or why we are doing what we are. Doubt can enter the mind and cloud our path. It is no longer a path of joy if we have forgotten our highest desire. It is difficult to emerge from confusion if we keep drowning in self-doubt.

The heart knows more than the mind. If our attention favours the seriousness of the mind, we will stay lost in the cloud of conceptualisation and fantasy. Clarity is a welcome friend that clears the clouds so you can see what you want more than anything. Clarity and devotion are tied together and lead to the highest peace. What you want is an important question to ask so you can move from being a freedom-seeker to a freedom-finder. What are you devoted to?

As a human, I have not always been clear (to be honest, I have mostly been confused), but as Maharishi Krishnanada Ishaya says, "Confusion is the last defence of the ego." Since I have been confused so much of my life, I must have been closer to enlightenment than I thought. Clarity was not something that stuck around me; it seemed to mysteriously sneak up on me when I became aware of the path of joy. The more devoted to peace I became, the more I could see everything in the bright clear light. As a result, my doubts became easier to see through, and I paid less attention to the chattering mind.

This is also related to the famous split desires that I had heard Maharishi mention once. Making a decision about going on a meditation retreat for a few months was driving me crazy; I couldn't decide if I wanted to go or not. It was a big decision because I knew I might be there for a long time (probably because I felt as if I had a mountain of stress to clear out). I called a teacher at the retreat to talk about the problem, and he said, "You just have a split desire," and suggested to forget about coming for the moment and see what happened. My mind was suddenly out of a job. Both desires and the struggle between them ("should I

stay or should I go?") let go on their own. Virtually instanta-
neously, everything became very clear, and I realised what I
wanted. I was using confusion to avoid what I already knew in
my heart. It was still hard for me to leave my familiar life at the
time, but the direction I would take was now more obvious, and
I felt less doubt.

What happens when a person with advanced surrendering
master 108th degree meditation skills is still totally confused?
Using the skills in the art of devotion, I asked myself, "What am
I devoted to?" Oh, yes, I am devoted to making the silence the
most important thing—*clarity at last!*

Clarity is infinite. Sure, it's not enlightenment, but it is nice to
see the path you are on so you don't get bitten by the *chupacabras*
(bloodsuckers or doubts) along the side of the road. Clarity is a
welcome light that just gets brighter and brighter until no doubts
can challenge that brilliance.

As devotion peels back the layers, we can settle into a sweet,
unmoving certainty. This devotion is absolutely without effort; it
is calm and gigantic, as well as simple and powerful. It has
within it the sweet momentum of love which, like a joyful
hurricane, cannot be forced or controlled. When it's got you,
you're toast.

Contentment

Being completely content with where we are right now is a rare thing. Without contentment, we will always be trying to change our experience to get a better, shinier one. Separate individuals desire to be better and will never be satisfied because their nature is to seek out a different experience from the one that is happening right now. What is happening now is never enough.

Paradoxically, what is happening now is the invitation to contentment, the seed to losing ourselves in the silence. What is happening now is the vehicle for liberation; it is an opportunity for grace, surrender, and fulfillment.

By actively exploring, we see clearly that the silence is eternally content and has no desire to change the changeless or what is happening now. This lack of desire for change is the contentment we long for. We need add nothing to ourselves in order to be complete. There is nothing missing in what we are, yet when we engage the conceptualising mind, we can find a list of things to add or subtract from life. Why not begin by subtracting the act of conceptualising itself? The root of the problem is conceptualising. The answer is to laugh at it.

Right now you are reading these words. This is it. But is reading just happening or are you doing it? Don't think about it— just be curious and laugh at yourself.

We continue as if something is indeed missing, always seeking the next high. Are we spiritual addicts chasing down our next fix? Why can't we just stop and breathe? Relax and stay in the only place where there is contentment... *ourselves*.

The cosmic joke is that we are shifting and moving in what does not move. Looking for something other than what we are will never quench our thirst for happiness, yet this is what our restless minds do. Look *inward*, not outward. "Seek the kingdom of Heaven, and all else shall be added unto thee." By pointing our compass toward the silence of being, all else shall be added.

Everything will always be greater than our limited individual mind could have imagined—guaranteed!

Eventually, even looking for ourselves becomes a laugh. What is it that is looking inward for itself?

What is happening right now is all there is. What part of us would or could change anything? We have little control, if any, over what happens. Our only control is where we put our attention. The little me will never be fully satisfied with anything, but if it disappears, there is no question of fulfillment. We are complete at last because we are no longer seeking.

It is possible to have our attention resting so fully in the stillness that the desire to stay there overwhelms all our other desires, making them less attractive. Of course we still have desires, but they do not *own* us. Our happiness is not dependent on whether or not we fulfill our desires but only on where we place our attention. This is the wisdom in surrendering our desires and also in the saying, "If you want God to laugh, tell him your plans." If you really want God to laugh, find out who is laughing.

Ah, contentment! What more could you want?

Divine Will

You have done nothing wrong your whole life.
—Maharishi Krishnananda Ishaya

The silence of the path of joy heals the belief that something is wrong with our lives. I think it's easy to accept that right now I am doing nothing wrong. I am just sitting here and typing, so what possible wrong could come from that? Please don't tell me—I'm scared to find out! Oh, great—now you've got me thinking again. I can be so insecure sometimes.

It's a little harder to accept that I have never, ever, done anything wrong (in this life or past lives if you believe in them). When I first heard the words, "I have never done anything wrong," they made my heart sing, and I wanted to believe them. Still, of course, my energetic body didn't quite accept them even though my mind thought they sounded reasonable.

My sense was that "doing nothing wrong" had something to do with the way divine will and personal will was playing out in my life. I really didn't understand, yet intuitively I was aware that the choices I had made, good or bad, were less about me than I used to think. I had read that the puppet-self had its own programming, which it accepted through no fault of its own. This, of course, meant that some actions occur without an individual choice, or so I read.

In the past, instead of just using my intuition (the simple way), I would use my intellect to try to understand the age-old, spiritual question, "Is there free will or not?" Eventually, I saw that it's not really understanding that's important but knowing in your heart or gut. By the way, understanding "There is no free will" as a concept is a great way to get stuck in "mental enlightenment." It feels good to get stuck there because the ego feels so free to do what it wants since nothing matters anymore. It happens quite often to people on the path, including me. It takes some humility, a great teacher, or simply seeing that there is more to life than this intellectual position. It's simply another example of valuing an idea over the pure subjectivity of the silence.

One thing became very clear as I continued to surrender. The more I held onto the past, either as a thought or energetically in my body, the more I kept freedom at a distance. I thought, "How can I deserve eternal peace when I am comparing myself to the pure sages of the world? I am not even as pure as most people I pass on the street."

In my case it was easier to forgive others than myself. I harboured guilt about past actions that seemed to justify why I was not experiencing permanent peace. Even when I had no story to tell, I had that old feeling in my heart that I was not okay. I was walking around as if on eggshells, waiting to do something wrong and fearful of some imaginary punishment inflicted by a phantom authority. It was as if I was waiting for God and all the angels to come out, point their pure, light fingers at me, and say, "Look at how impure he is! He thinks he deserves enlightenment. What a loser!" Whatever the will of God was, I certainly didn't feel included in it. Looking back, I can see it was arrogant to think that I was special enough not to get included in the will. Don't you agree?

Divine will can be tricky to understand or describe, but as the personal will dissolves in favour of the silence, the unimaginable or difficult transforms into the easy and obvious. This basically means that by surrendering my will, my life will get easier and easier, and hence it will become a path of joy guided by divine will. Just when we think life couldn't get any easier, it does. That's the one thing Maharishi kept telling me. When I told him life was easy, he would say, "Just wait three months from now — you won't believe how difficult you made it." I have found that in gauging your experience to see how well you are doing, ask yourself, "How easy is it?" Then just make it easier! (Hint:

Meditation is easy, and thoughts are okay!)

If meditation becomes difficult, then your personal will is involved. How do I stop my personal will from manipulating everything including my meditation? That is the Zen of how. The simple answer is to keep exploring the stillness and forget everything else. That makes it easy.

What was eye-opening for me was letting go of the idea of needing more experiences to wake up. I felt I needed to cleanse my wrongs, secretly confess my sins, or purify myself. It felt as if my soul needed a serious karmic cleansing of all the stuff I had trapped inside. The problem was, I had a storage unit made up of memories, feelings, and concepts about the soul and karma that was big enough to keep me purifying forever. I asked a teacher in a meeting if I needed to keep having experiences so I would be ready for freedom, and he said, "No, absolutely not!" (I probably should have listened to that.) I felt that I just needed to help one more little grandma to cross the street, and then God would see that I was ready. The problem is, there are so many little grannies out there—not that there is anything wrong with them.

There is no question of worthiness when it comes to waking up. There is only the infinite presence of God, and you are that. We don't wake up right now because we feel unworthy of the whole enchilada, which seems like too much for us. Of course it's too much, and we can't handle it, but that is why we surrender the little will for the big one. The personal will can only manage personal things, and it even does a bad job of doing that. Now it's trying to manage God? Are you crazy? Can I really manage the infinite when I hit my head on things all the time? The divine will can manage every infinite detail. (Now here's an advanced concept: it always does anyway, even when we think *we're* doing it.)

You are in an ocean of infinite love, and in the middle is a tiny dot saying, "I'm not worthy of this!" For most people, this is a strong reason why freedom seems impossible. "Maybe I will work on myself for ten years, and then I'll be prepared," we say. But this moment never arrives, and then we die. Maybe we will wake up in Heaven when we die, but then again, maybe not. Let's not wait and find out.

Ultimately, we just want to be loved and to love ourselves. I think this is one of the best descriptions of enlightenment: "I love myself." That says it all. It doesn't say, "I love myself, but... "

Can you imagine how great it would be if you really loved yourself completely? I mean to the core of your being—everything about you, even all the dark stuff that you want to hide. The divine will is like a huge, brilliant light that loves everything. If you are not in Unity with all there is, it is because you still have a personal will and are unwilling to love yourself enough to give up to the divine the illusion that you have control. You may never have the will to love yourself, yet the divine will loves you completely. Surrendering to the silence leads to that love. The divine will loves you to death and then loves you some more.

Divine will takes you to divine love, where you are right now reading these words and have always been in this embrace of love. Nothing can change that. So jump, if that's the will of God!

Harmony

You carry the bubble with you wherever you go.
—Maharishi Krishnananda Ishaya

To be in harmony is the greatest way to be in the world but not of it. It sends a message that life is indeed wonderful and complete as it is. Being in harmony doesn't mean that we have only nice thoughts or that everyone around us is kissing each other, dancing, and handing out flowers (though I've noticed that kissing and dancing happens more in some places than others, like Mexico for example). We are much more likely to have some drama around us, as well as a mixed variety of nuts, so to speak, if we live in the city. (Maybe you are a little nutty too.)

In unconditional harmony, life flows effortlessly without putting importance on the variety of forms life takes. As consciousness expands, our perception evolves to embrace life with gentleness and ease. This happens naturally as we learn to make the unchanging self more important than the dancing play of changes. Let's be honest; everything changes all the time. I've always found that part of life the most difficult. I like things to be the same because, for me, sameness has always symbolised safety and security. (Okay, I can be a bit boring, but at least I am safe and sound amid the nuts out there.)

Sameness was why I secretly wanted to wander off into the forest or disappear into the mountains. When I was younger, I would fantasise about living with the Tibetan monks. I saw myself in the Himalayas, seeing the magical sages I had read about. My thinking typified the saying, "The grass is always greener on the other side of the fence." I was searching for my bubble. If I had seen a Tibetan monk walking by in robes in Calgary, I would have passed out or screamed like a little girl seeing a member of a boy band. The area I live in now has a highly diverse population, and it is not uncommon to see monks walking around. I wouldn't scream or faint anymore, however.

When I was in the Himalayas, I was with a swami, and as he shared stories from the Vedas, I was in awe. While he was talking, one of his students came by after a long trip through the mountains to visit with the yogis up in the caves. The swami said to him, "Tell him of all your great adventures visiting the sages!" I looked at him with rapt attention, waiting to soak up his stories. He was a chubby fellow with a chubby face who was munching on a banana. He looked at me and looked at his teacher. I could tell he was searching for something interesting to say, but he just shrugged his shoulders and said it was okay. Embarrassed, the swami rolled his eyes and changed the subject. He probably was so used to living among the yogis that it was no big deal.

For a period of my life, I lived in harmony almost at every instant. I was living with monks at a retreat center in Mexico, and there was virtually no drama or stress at all (unless you made fun of Baby Jesus—then you were sent to the corner). The focus was on exploring the silence and sharing in the discovery of that together. We were on the path of joy. Can you imagine what that was like? It was wonderful, like living in Heaven on earth. Hugs and smiles and the sacredness of love were commonplace all day long.

Even though this supporting bubble was overflowing with harmony, sometimes things would change in my life (like the end of a relationship) that would challenge the flow I was experiencing with the environment. Change would happen when I became too complacent or arrogant that nothing could shake my peace. It seemed I could not hide from my own destiny. (God would never give a warning notice of things to come, either.) Ironically, I used to pray to God to send me anything that would destroy my ego and bring about freedom. Can I take that back now?

Sometimes the bubble started to look more inharmonious. Our subjective relationship with ourselves is immediately reflected on the outside, bubble or not. In other words, harmony on the inside equals harmony on the outside. In this case, the disharmony on the outside seemed to threaten the stability of my peace.

I was reminded that through focusing on the unchanging formless, I could allow form to change without letting it affect my peace. Indeed, form always does change; it's just that we get caught in the middle of this natural dance. The formless and form dance to a song that is not personal, even when it seems very much so.

These changes in form are always humbling to witness. Now I know I have no control over events on the outside. I prefer things I am enjoying in life to stay the same; however, I am also open to what divine will has in store. History has taught me that living in this uncontrolled openness always leads to the highest good. The more I try to change the inevitable, the more I fuel chaos.

I consider myself very fortunate to have had some time to go inward and to have spent time chatting with amazing teachers and monks. I am the most grateful for the time when I left the bubble and headed out into the world. I remember how excited I was. (Adyashanti calls this the "spiritual rubber hitting the road.")

I went from being in a bubble of smiles, hugs, and consciousness to working as a roofer in London, Ontario, with violent drug addicts, ex-convicts, and just plain, mean old puppets. What happened to the harmony of the path of joy? I missed my harmony bubble. I wanted my mommy (though I didn't say that because I am too tough).

Peace is not outside in the world—it is inside! So is harmony. It does not matter what happens in daily life because we can always move our attention to the path of joy. Of course, it helps when you surround yourself with fresh popcorn—not stale, mouldy, and greasy kernels. (No offence to my old co-workers.)

Our environment does have an energetic influence, yet what we are is absolutely bigger than that influence. After being surrounded by negativity all day, I would sometimes drive home, frowning, my shoulders and body tense. I could feel where the stress of the day had built up (especially in my gut). Then a moment of awareness would come. "What is going on?" I'd think. Then laughter would arise at the contrasting energy in my body. I would "hit the reset button and start over." I affectionately call this stress "roofer stress." You can take on the energy of whatever your work bubble happens to be— accounting stress if you are an accountant or meditation stress if you are a monk. (Don't forget, there is a lot of pressure to get enlightened if you are a monk. This is the worst kind of stress because you never get truly enlightened, even after many lifetimes.)

I remember the first moment when my harmony bubble of peace started to crack. One of the guys at work (I called him my dark angel) was getting on my nerves so badly that I walked away and started mumbling out loud, "That son of a... " I was watching myself take the energy seriously instead of letting it move (which is totally okay, by the way). I noticed it and thought, "Wow, look at that—I'm talking to myself out loud." I couldn't remember the last time I'd talked out loud to myself, but there it was. You see, it's enough to just watch and allow. Allowing alone will help redirect your attention to the path of joy. Of course, if you'd screamed and yelled instead, there would have been no difference. Emotions are energy in motion, so let 'em rip.

The body (energetic puppet body) just naturally responds to the environment it is in. The reaction is not a personal vendetta against you; it's just the body reacting to the stress in the air. What doesn't help is thinking about it. Instead, practise *ahimsa* (non-violence). Don't take it seriously. Breathe.

What would happen if you picked up an enlightened sage

and put him in your shoes? How would he behave? What would he feel or do? The sage looks, behaves, and feels exactly like you if you allow it all. The puppet is a puppet. The only difference is the sage doesn't need to change, nor does he have a desire to change, what moves inside and outside the energetic puppet body. Energy changes, but the sage resting in the silence stays with his attention on the formless. This is harmony.

When we are aware, we can move in the direction of silence. Start fresh and innocently, take a deep breath, and recommit to your peace and harmony, which is way more important than what happened at work or while meditating in the cave—let it go!

In seeking harmony, it helps to take time to plug back into stillness and the path of joy. If what you are doing to experience peace is not working for you, try something else. Stay open to the grace of the universe. If peace is important to you, the universe will give you everything you need, including the best meditation tools to help you live in harmony. I can recommend some tools, but you have to make the choice between thinking or harmony. Who cares what he or she said to you or what you said or did— *it's over!*

The beauty of experiencing working with someone who is over-the-top nuts is that now I can work with anyone. Even the hardest guy to work with is a sweet, gentle angel in comparison. Anytime I am in a difficult environment and people are complaining, I remember my roofing stress and smile... it could be worse.

Rest, relax, and enjoy the gift of harmony... life is too short.

Immortality

Know and accept that immortality is only the shining of the true clarity (i.e. Pure Consciousness), without the delusion of mental modification. Death cannot be overcome by anything other than that pure consciousness.
—Sri Muruganar

Our true nature is immortality. Throughout history (my own included), immortality has come to be defined superficially as "the body living forever." When I was younger, this concept appealed to me. Reading books like *Autobiography of a Yogi* were inspiring and made me believe anything was possible with the right amount of effort. The miraculous looked like manifesting things out of thin air, bi-locating, or being invisible. I wished I could have been invisible many times; it would have saved me some embarrassment.

Ultimately, we come to the conclusion that what is miraculous is that we still don't know what we are. It is a miracle that the one can hide itself as the many. But the impossible is made possible, thanks to the mysterious maya (illusion) apparently happening on the surface of this oneness. The infinite one performs a magician's trick to become separate to itself.

I hate to admit it, but there was a time in my life when I was very superficial and vain. I could not pass a mirror without looking at it. Maybe I thought I was too handsome to be mortal, so I sought out ways to become immortal, such as, yoga, meditation, magic herbs, living off light, etc., to grace you and the world forever with my sexy body and angelic face. You don't have to thank me; it was my pleasure. Living forever was my mission until it dawned on me that living forever in this body might not actually be the great achievement I thought it was. (It would probably be boring as hell.) And I guess there was more to life than being ridiculously good-looking.

As the superficial was replaced with the powerful desire to know the truth, exploring the stillness became the way to immortality. The more I focused on what does not change, the less I desired the miraculous, and the more miraculous everyday life became. Suddenly, simple things like eating cereal or laughing became extraordinary.

Continuing with this exploration, the silence radiated with the brilliance of eternal light. It was filling everything up in its path, including the mortal self. The world of duality and transience transformed itself into a Heaven of divine beauty and bliss. The body, the trees, the sky, and the mountains became a still painting of immortality infused with life and more real than ever, now that there was not a separate person trying to escape mortality. I could see that forms were the moving colours of the formless self. That the colours would move and dance on the tapestry of God's immortal life brought tears of awe as this clarity intensified.

What we are is immortal, which is beyond death and change. The body will die (change form), but the adventure is in letting go of the fear of death, which has its root in identifying with the body. (I *am* my body.) Everything that is not you comes and goes—it is born and then dies. Thoughts come out of nowhere and die into nothing. Emotions come out of nothing and disappear into nowhere. You see this dance of change rising and falling away in a natural witnessing of the silence. Only to the separate individual does it seem like a tragedy that the body dies.

What is comical is that everything that we think we are dies all the time, hundreds of times a day. Whenever we are enjoying something to the fullest, our identity/ego disappears in the active enjoyment. We don't notice it because the ego no longer matters or is lessimportant than what our attention is focused on. The puppet dissolves into the background and is no longer a part of our reality. From the silence, we can witness the puppet as it rises and falls away in the context of awareness.

We can be consciously aware of this absence (disappearing in the silence). This happens on the path of joy during meditation. Whenever our sense of self dies, we are automatically in the immortal presence of God. The more we explore this, the more we see that it is not some new state. It is ordinary because it is all there is and a familiar experience. But it is extraordinary because it is so absolutely alive that it is miraculous we never noticed it before. Absolute magic!

Einstein says, "Energy cannot be created or destroyed, it can only be changed from one form to another." There you have the entire key to immortality. Through attention on what doesn't change form, you don't change form. Through attention on the unborn, you are unborn. Yet without warning, our attention wanders, and suddenly we are form again as we become caught up in the whirlwind of the mind. This is just the habit of the auto-puppet. So what? It's a game. Even death is just another concept floating around in our head. What would happen if that concept were to die?

If we are willing to play and explore to see what is immortal, then true immortality will be revealed. If the revelation takes a little time, it's only because the Self thinks it's funny to watch the puppet take this game so seriously. This Immortal Self might seem to trick you by taking your attention off on adventures, but only out of fun and enjoyment of the game. God has a terrible sense of humour.

Besides immortality, ideas of superpowers are very appealing in today's culture. Who doesn't want to be Superman, Superwoman or a "supersage" like Jesus? It's interesting to note that in literature, the sage or "enlightened person" has adopted many of the superhero's attributes. Who wouldn't want the ability to change water into Coke or even into herbal tea if you are a pure puppet?

I have spent much of my life fascinated with the story of the supersage as an ideal to chase after. I tried to strengthen my supersage muscles by practising the greatest of all techniques like the one mentioned in *Autobiography of a Yogi*. In fact, I met a sage in India who taught me this technique. His students were all superhero crazy as they told me of all the miraculous things they had witnessed this supersage perform. I felt crazy with anticipation and thought, "Give me some of that superness!"

This supersage told me that I would have many visions. He said that "Jesus had practised this technique." His students also told me that they had seen him disappear before their eyes and bi-locate, and that his teacher was a three hundred-year-old yogi living in a cave somewhere.

I began to practise with an intense desire for the miraculous. When I found it, I was happy. When I saw the lights, and fireworks, and the blue sphere I was happy. When I could feel my cells pulsating with light, I was happy. None of these experiences lasted, however, and when they disappeared, all I was left with was my inflated yogi puppet (which looked like Kermit the frog in lotus position). Sure, it looked as if I was climbing higher up on the ladder, but peace was nowhere up there. (It was probably back on the ground.) This lack of peace became clearer to me later as I was talking to the teacher about this experience.

There was a contrast between the silence of the path of joy, which was simply peaceful, and my supersage idea, which was loud, exciting, yet somehow hollow. The teacher said, "You have the ability to rest in the absolute source of everything. What part of you would want to do anything else?"

My superhero-wannabe ego hated that! I loved working on my supersage image! How else was I going to be special? I didn't have any other talents or skills, but I could be a flying, non-eating, teleporting yogi. What he said resonated in my heart, but I didn't want to give up my specialness. If I wasn't special, what was I? After flipping between chasing experiences versus settling into the pure subjectivity of all that is, I experienced clarity.

There is no "enlightened person." A person wants to be special and is more attracted to the superpowers than the infinite source because then the ego feels worthy. As long as we believe that the supersage is anything more than entertainment, we avoid the reality of the sage. The sage has lost the separate person and is void of ego or specialness. The sage is pure humility because no one is putting on a show anymore. When you *are* pure attention, you don't need attention.

I am not saying that a sage sometimes doesn't have super-powers; I am sure he can and does have them. What I *am* saying is that a present sage doesn't crave and chase after those experiences. A very wise sage once said that you can have all those miracle powers with an ego still in place, but the only thing you can't have with an ego is the Immortal Self.

You are already immortal—you don't need to show off!

Present Moment

It is on God's purpose, hidden in the cloud of all that happens to you in the present moment, that you must rely. You will find that it always surpasses your own wishes. The present moment holds infinite riches beyond your wildest dreams.
—Jean-Pierre de Caussade

Infinite riches! Maximum enjoyment! Sounds good... mmm... yummy.

Shanti and I are fans of Eckhart Tolle. I read *The Power of Now* when it first came out, and it was exactly what I was looking for at the time. It is all about being in the now, which happens as we live in the silence and don't take the past and future seriously. I tried pretty hard to live in the now until it was explained to me that the silence is the source of the now and not the other way around. Now it is effortless to "be here now." In truth, is there any other option while exploring the silence?

Recently, we were having a silly conversation about how rich Eckhart Tolle is. Shanti was saying that you don't get rich writing books. But I said, "No way—he's rolling in it." I can't open up a web page anymore without his face popping up. When I am surfing the Web, he is a very good reminder about being present. We were talking about it because we had been listening to one of his talks in which he shared that he still sometimes lives like he did before he had all the money. It must be pretty funny checking out price tags when you have a massive budget.

One Sunday as we were crossing a street, Shanti started poking and grabbing at me saying, "Look, look, it's Eckhart Tolle, look, look." So I turned my head, and sure enough, there he was, sitting in the now in his brand new, light blue Jaguar. As he sat at the lights, he had both hands on the wheel and was as present as ever.

The point is, it is not only about being in the now. If you are right about something and the universe believes in you, it will send a blue jaguar to show your partner you were right! Being in the moment is just a nice side bonus.

Even Eckhart Tolle can let go of his old habits around money. That's one more image of a sage destroyed.

Obviously, being poor or rich financially has nothing to do with freedom. The positions we hold onto, however, can hold us back from the fullness of now. This applies no matter how conscious we may appear. The freer we are, the more humility and willingness we have to see what we are holding onto. To a sage, seeing that position is not personal anymore—it is simply more liberating. Maybe it's about the collective consciousness of the planet and not about me—who knows?

The universe will always reflect what we are holding onto. If we are listening, it becomes very obvious. If not, just ask someone what they see you holding onto.

Having debt used to be frustrating to me. I remember having $1500 on my credit card and being worried sick about paying it off. Then, at $3000, I thought, "That's it. I need to pay this off. It's getting out of control." At the time I was helping out at a retreat centre for six months in Mexico and six months in Canada. My mind would be present, and then it would start wandering off, thinking about debt. Whenever I went shopping, I would look at the price tag and would remember my balance. I was making very little money at the time, but I also liked nice shoes, so what was I going to do? Be responsible?

I found a job outside of the centre to help pay off this debt, but at the end of the year my credit card balance was at $7000 dollars. Nothing I was doing was working. (I know. I should have just stopped using the card.) Money was my special sticky thought. I needed a miracle.

Often the teachers would talk about freedom. I wanted freedom, but I needed shoes. While thinking about my credit card one day, I laughed because it occurred to me how much time I was spending thinking about money instead of staying alert to the beauty of now. But thinking about it was not paying off my balance. I knew that if I stopped using it and made large payments, I would pay it off eventually. Not being present was not helping anything at all. I was choosing thinking and fantasising over being present. The topic was money, but it could have been anything else that I was making more important than freedom.

These patterns around money were old. I could write a book on all the money talk I'd heard growing up. Lack, lack, lack. Quack, quack, quack—don't get me started. Once I saw what I was doing, I decided to pick freedom over the thoughts. I wish I could tell you that a miracle happened and I received a cheque in the mail for $7000 from an unknown relative, but that happened to another lucky fella.

What happened was my bills got higher until they reached the maximum level I could handle without freaking out. When the balance passed that level, I would go into fear mode and start thinking again. When it reached $10,000, I panicked and then chose freedom while my mind said, "Well, at least it's not $13,000. That would be ridiculous—you'd never be able to pay that amount off."

It is exciting to discover new places that keep us from being in the present and enjoying life to the maximum. This frees up more space in our awareness for freedom to flourish.

Through a continued, renewed interest in exploring what is real *now*, an unlimited adventure unfolds, always revealing a greater and more subtle enjoyment of this moment. The beauty of this practice is that the enjoyment of the still presence overshadows anything else, which becomes irrelevant to what is happening in the present moment. Drinking a cup of tea, seeing a movie, falling down the stairs, or whatever happens, is happening within a great freedom to enjoy this moment. And "ouch" is a reminder to be present when walking down the stairs.

Living in the now allows for a snowball effect; momentum builds, which increases the natural and effortless ability of our attention to appreciate the underlying reality. This makes it easy to anchor into the stillness, allowing for the shifting play of life to dance on, unencumbered.

It's quite magical to notice that while enjoying the silence, the little things we like in life become even more enjoyable. A cup of coffee just tastes better. As well, the things we would prefer not to happen, such as falling down the stairs, are less tragic. Even those events we dislike are surrounded by the ever-present joy of attention on what does not change. The momentum of enjoying the silence of reality has a magical power that enlivens our ability to enjoy the show.

I met a sage once who had MS. She had less and less control over her body as the disease progressed and would sometimes fall over. To the surprise of those around her, she would just start laughing. Then everyone around her would also start to laugh. She wasn't taking the events happening personally and was teaching us not to be serious. This was an inspiration.

As the momentum builds, life starts to show us when we are thinking about things unnecessarily or just not being very present. These are little gifts that come as reminders. They are not by chance. If you start to use them as opportunities to reconnect with the silence, they become incredible tools. They usually become gentler than getting smacked in the head as your choice to be present becomes more important.

If you are committed wholeheartedly to being present, then life sends you Eckhart Tolle in a blue Jaguar as a reminder. If not, then you get hit by the Jaguar—ouch!

One of my favourite reminders came when I was with a fellow student and we were flying down a hill in a badly beat-up, old Dodge. My side of the door was barely hanging onto the truck. I was in the passenger seat holding the door closed and was thinking about my life and all my problems. Suddenly, my friend decided to make a sharp left turn because he'd forgotten something, and I flew out of the truck, along with a big glass water bottle, and landed on my ass. I started to laugh because instantly I was alert and alive to this moment. All my useless thinking and analysing was over.

Usually, it's hitting my head on things or a fly that just won't go away that reminds me. When we don't take things seriously, we can allow life to keep showing us more ways to be fully alive. The alternative is to stay in auto-puppet mode and wear a helmet.

Purity

What does it mean to be pure? How can we achieve a high level of purity?

Here are some ideas: taking vitamins; meditating more; thinking less; being still; not judging ourselves or judging ourselves for judging; allowing more; surrendering more; giving more; praising more; drinking filtered water; stretching more; cleansing; detoxing; letting go; breathing more deeply; doing more energy work; reading more spiritual books; talking to the angels, not eating that second doughnut; telling the truth; being kind to animals, plants, and humans; forgiving your mother; and taking blue-green algae.

But even if we do all these things, what are we purifying? What is the point? Where are we going? Don't get me wrong; I love doing energy work, being kind to plants and insects, and currently am eating blue-green algae.

I used to think if I did all those things and more I would master purity. But what happens is that the purity of the silence unfolds continuously despite what we decide to do. The magic of purity is that it *is* what we are despite how we act or what we do.

It's impossible to tell if any act was done out of purity just by observing the act itself. From the silence, however, all is pure and is mastered because the Self is pure—not me, you, or any separate thing.

I am not saying that any action is a pure action, but I am saying that not only the actions themselves determine purity. When we rest in purity, all actions are automatically pure no matter what they look like. Obviously, an evil action is probably being done by someone who is not resting in silence or on a path of joy. But when all ideas vanish in favour of the Self, what will the sage do? What will you do? What would Jesus do?

Will all ideas of a pure life instantly manifest when we master purity? Absolutely not. From the silence, allowing what is happening now is the purest expression of purity. This comes from the infinite when the separate puppet is out of the way. Life is pure and simple when we dissolve in the silence.

Regardless of the past, what we have done, and how impure we have seemed, when we turn our attention to the purity of the silence, we are instantly pure *now*.

I used to have respect for spiritual teachers in proportion to how purely they had lived their lives (based on my purity gauge) and the greatest respect for those born awake in totally purity. When I found a skeleton in the closet, some of that respect would turn into doubt. Now my point of view has flipped. I have the utmost respect for those regular folk who have approached the path of the sages with courage from the most impure of lives. They are true inspirations for us all. They resonate into the core of our being, reflecting unconditional love. They say, "If I can do it, so can you."

After all, how would the path of joy be about unconditional love if not every single one of us, regardless of our pasts, could recognise that freedom? Whether or not the puppet seems pure or impure is irrelevant, in Unity all there is, is purity... Our ignorance of our true nature doesn't change the purity of it. The truth is, we have sages of all backgrounds and experiences, and this variety of flavours is a testament to the impartial love of oneness, a purity of unity.

Wisdom

Ah, the dreaded ego monster. Oh, how I have longed for your destruction! But what is it am I trying to destroy anyway? What is the ego? When doing some research on this monster, you come up with hundreds of definitions from psychology, Buddhism, and Christianity. A big book could and probably has been written on all these ideas.

They say to keep your friends close and your enemies even closer, but how can we get close enough to destroy the ego when nobody really knows what it is in the first place? Understanding it intellectually does not weaken it, but is trying to destroy it feasible? Is it even possible, or are we just spending all our time and energy on nothing at all? Maybe the ego is inflating instead of deflating.

The ego has a bad rap in some circles, but when we do a little inner inspection (starting innocently, without any ideas about what the ego is), we realise it's not that bad. As we go inward, into the stillness, we see the whole process of what happens beyond the mind and ego. It helps to take a step back and get a good view, which can bring about clarity and simplify the whole journey for us if we want. Of course, a better way is to make it all about the silence *now*, but that is way too easy for some of us.

Even if Buddha were doing the talking, it is not enough for us to just trust what someone says—we need to find out for ourselves. Direct experience is the quickest way to become free from the ego because we know first-hand what works. We know in the core of our being instead of from hearing about it or reading about it in *Killing Ego* magazine. Knowing what works from firsthand experience puts us in a better position to be our own authority. This is not an ego-based authority in which we are in charge of the process but a selfless knowing of what is useful on the path of joy. This is wisdom.

What we notice about the operation of me, self, ego, or sense of self can be very liberating but also very frustrating if we get entangled in conceptualising. When trying to get rid of our egos for some goal (enlightenment or self-improvement), interest and energy can appear to inflate it. Just a quick taste of silence can transform individuals and therefore their egos. The ego can continue to overinflate an experience so we can appear special in the world. This is obviously an attempt to fill an endless hole. The apparent danger to the innocence of the seeker is that we can get easily caught up in teachings or teachers who speak about "the spiritual truth." This does not mean the information is not coming from a pure place, only that we always have the potential to conceptualise. It is important to understand what we are dealing with. It is simple.

This is the age of information; we can know anything we want. Nobody on the planet has to even know anything anymore—just google it! This is wonderful but also confuses the seeker because of an overload of spiritual information and misinformation. Transcending this information is the energetic power of the popcorn effect, which completely bypasses all of this information. It happens out of the grace of resonance. The heart is not a huge fan of information; it just wants to taste the bliss. The proof of the pudding is in the eating of it. The heart doesn't stop until it moves through all the BS. Sure, we get stuck in weird places; I spent years involved with those who spoke the truth, literally word for word. I could not have said it better, yet something was off. The alive experience is all that matters. Discernment develops with experience. Pretty soon you become like a laser that cuts through the most slippery and subtle ideas.

If the ego is the source of our problems, it seems logical to target it for extinction to get what we want. Usually the idea is expressed like this: "If I get rid of this 'me,' then I will be at peace." This "getting rid of" idea is used by the me/ego/self or the "mego" self (you can't have enough terms to describe the ego) in a thousand different ways. If I get rid of my judging, I will be happier, more liked, and master of myself. This creates the vicious judging-myself-for-judging cycle. If I get rid of this anxiety, I will be complete; this thought maintains the anxiety because of the interest in it. These examples show the great circular way of the mego—it keeps delaying the peace that it is actually claiming to help achieve by getting rid of things. You're a clever little mego, aren't you!

Thoughts, feelings, and our sense of self comes and goes. Whenever we are enjoying the movie without being absorbed in the character, the mego is gone. What about getting rid of the character? The character or puppet is not the problem. Even in unity, the puppet is still there with its own characteristics and programming. Actually, your essence or expression is now fully here and shining like never before.

One puppet might like butter on the popcorn and the other not. In unity, our identification with the puppet is gone. The puppet still has a flavour and personality (unless it's a vegetable puppet) as it moves around on the stage, but the mego is not there. The puppet is an appearance only, just another part of the movie. Since you cannot have a movie without a character, you have no choice about whether the puppet is there, or not. If it is not there then that means you are reading this in heaven. (Just pinch yourself to check.) You can have a movie without a mego, however, and that is the important distinction. In fact this mego-less state is the best way to enjoy the show! The mego is like an unwanted actor jumping into a role that doesn't even exist.

Through observing and not analysing, we observe that the mego is just a bunch of thoughts that come and go. Why do anything with the mego when it is just a naturally occurring phenomenon arising and subsiding like any thought? We place importance on it because we see it as the last enemy, but this is only a crazy idea, not based in reality.

During sleep or when we are experiencing stillness, it is not there. Then a thought comes: "I want to stay here, so I need to get rid of this mego." If we see this thought simply as the play of the waves on the ocean, then there is no battle and no problem. If there is a problem, then guess what? It's the mego's problem. We are thinking and taking things seriously again. What part of us would do that? That's right—the mego.

It is more valuable to focus on the stillness. Through the inward power of the big Self, we come to see through the story, the veils, and the mego with absolute ease that is sprinkled with humour and acceptance. The path of joy is a path of laughing at ourselves. The mego isn't really there anyway, especially when we are laughing. At the very least, we shouldn't take this investigation seriously.

The fire of wisdom burns through the illusions of the mego. It cannot get rid of the mego because there is no mego at all. The wisdom sees that no effort is required to remove a mirage. Trying to negotiate with a phantom is pointless.

Speaking of phantoms, when I was in Mexico, we were staying at a five hundred-year-old hacienda with a very rich and sometimes violent history. Some of the students would see ghosts. One day, a lady said she saw one in my room floating in the corner. I was getting annoyed with all these ghosts and finally snapped, thinking this ghost might even be a pervert. I thought, "Jesus, we are running a retreat here. Why don't you just go away?"

While the lady was there, I said to the ghost, "Do you not have something better to do? Why don't you move on with your life instead of hanging around here? There is more to life than floating around watching us!"

The ghost replied, "I have more right to be here than you—I was here long before you were!"

"You have a point," I said. I made friends with the ghost, but from then on I would get dressed in the bathroom just in case.

Perhaps when we stop trying to get rid of the ego, the struggle will be transformed into a joyous exploration of what is real, in which there is maximum enjoyment of the stillness, and where nothing is serious and the mego is the star attraction of the cosmic joke.

Forget all this mego and mego-less nonsense and keep on the path of joy. Oh, look—there goes my mego!

A Path of Joy

Eternal Moment

That which is called happiness is only the nature of Self; Self
is not other than perfect happiness. That which is called
happiness alone exits. Knowing that fact abiding in that state
of Self, enjoy bliss eternally.
Sri Muruganar

In one instant I was looking backwards and forwards in time,
peering deeply into the past and the future. All I could see in both
directions was an eternal moment. In that moment there was
never suffering. All suffering only appeared to be happening
outside of eternity—it was happening to the conceptual "me"
who was stuck in time.

Then and during my enlightening "experience," I didn't have
even an idea of what it was like to suffer. In this concept-less
moment, I had difficulty remembering a single story about
suffering, let alone believing in it. You would have had to remind
me of what it was like. When had I suffered? When I look out at
the world, I see only this unity and cannot fathom why everyone
is not basking in the obvious treasure of what they are. I assume
you are basking in this unless you tell me otherwise.

For some time, I had to pretend I had suffered in order to
relate with people. I felt like both a liar and a comedian for good
reason—suffering was certainly not my experience. Then I
watched as one by one, specific events from my past would
present themselves in order to create a connection with those
who thought they were suffering. This emergence of events was
always spontaneously triggered and presently remembered.
Then I began to see the wisdom in the apparent process of
awakening in time. It called to mind what my meditation teacher
had said when I asked him why I was going through this: "Only

to help others," he said. Now all the crazy steps I had taken in my life made sense. The extremely personal was transformed into the impersonal.

In this eternal moment, those who I felt had hurt me in time were now my most beloved friends. We all play our roles perfectly. I even have a compassionate affection for the most painful stories as they come up. They seem to have happened to someone else or in a dream. In some cases they are grace in disguise, which fills me with gratitude. These stories are just like movies or educational videos that make us laugh, cry, or learn, yet it is only for entertainment or instruction that we watch them. They are not to be taken seriously. Why not pretend that none of them are ours? And wouldn't it be funny if all our stories existed only to make ourselves and other people laugh—except for the tragic ones, of course, which are for helping others get over their stories.

I spent a few years making my will to get enlightened more important than the silence. Welcome to the frustrating story of my life. (It's all about me.) Trying hard is what the ego does well. It loves to struggle, and the harder it tries, the more worthy and at the same time, the more cheated it feels (since it never actually gets what it wants). The good news is that we can surrender it all now.

As we explore the stillness, it becomes more obvious that the *now* is the perfect place to get stuck in time. When we stay here, we realise that the past and future stories are only ideas floating around in consciousness; they only appear to exist in the immensity of this eternal moment. Depending on our view, this moment appears tiny or incredibly huge.

The world of time is attached to our puppet, and as long as we identify with the puppet as "me," we are enslaved to the story happening in time. This shrinks eternity into a tiny present moment sandwiched between the past and future. This is one perception of a moment. It's a slice of pie but not the whole pie.

The silence and this eternal moment are one. Out of the stillness, this instant acts like a window into the great mystery of *now*. This instant is a very tiny part of a window into a much greater divine moment. When we are in the silence, this now is actually much greater than we had ever realised and much more profound. This is exciting! The amazing discovery is that this moment moves from a single sliver in time to an eternal ocean without limit. It's not important that we understand this eternal moment (I never have) but that we listen and stay open to the wonder and magic of it as it unfolds. If we let it, I am sure it will amaze us!

It is a joyous realisation that we cannot change this big *now*. All we can do is see its changeless treasure. Often we will take a break from actively engaging in the path of joy to hold onto a position. The more conscious we become, the more "enlightened" and "true" our positions appear to be. Having someone to guide us is valuable since the mind gets subtler and subtler. At points along the journey, it becomes difficult to see that we have any positions left at all. Anything held onto is limiting, even if it looks like the truth. That which *is* does not need to be maintained by claiming anything. Claiming is like planting your own truth flag in the absolute; now you have a flag but at the expense of the source of truth.

Living without positions opens up the infinite possibilities of our multi-dimensional nature, now beautifully described by current physicists. How can the mind comprehend the immensity of the eternal sphere? I guess that's why it is beyond the mind. This fact makes the path of joy very exciting!

I once had a great chat with a meditation teacher named Omkara that helped me see the joy of holding nothing (no matter how great it may seem) in this eternal moment. I loved listening to this monk who also happens to be a physicist. Many of us who explore the silence don't necessarily understand that world—not that we need to.

What he told us was that some of the current theories about quantum mechanics or ideas about how the infinite functions in the universe (understood intellectually) were now being transformed into an aliveness or reality beyond what the ideas were pointing to. (I am paraphrasing, of course, because I don't speak physicist.)

While talking to him one day, I saw that I was holding onto a limited idea about what is. He was talking about the infinite, potential possibilities of the eternal moment when I saw something. I could have sworn that I was not holding anything, but in an instant I saw it. The idea I was holding onto seemed so big and infinite that I assumed it was the absolute truth, and therefore, I had accepted it as "real." But even the absolute truth is not *the* absolute.

Seeing what we are holding onto can happen at any moment. It can happen while listening to your favourite music, doing the dishes, or riding a bike. It happens most often in the presence of a teacher and in the company of the wise. An attitude of exploration and a willingness to stay open encourages it.

Holding nothing is the great gateway to the infinite mystery of eternity.

Bliss

One's own reality (Self) which shines within everyone as Heart, is the ocean of unalloyed bliss. Therefore misery, which is unreal like the blueness of the sky, truly does not exist except in mere imagination.
Sri Muruganar

The path of joy is an exploration of the unknown. As we begin in humility and innocence with each facet of silence, the unknown reveals the universe and each facet as a universe within it. The unknown is empty of mind and full of heart—it is naked with openness. But what do I know? If being naked was all it took to make us more enlightened, then we could just go to a nude beach to wake up.

Seriously though, when we allow the energy of the unknown to be whatever it is, we settle into unknown bliss. The purest bliss has no cause and cannot be seen as an object. This bliss is completely selfless because it is without a reference point to our identity. There is no logical reason for this bliss to exist. It has no cause. It simply is.

We cannot see it because it is so close to what we are. Sometimes we see its reflection, just as we see our face in the mirror, yet in its true nature, it remains faceless. Like the eye that cannot see itself, it remains so obvious that it seems to hide from us. It is still, unmoving bliss or *satchitananda*. It is not just *satchit* (stillness/consciousness) with sprinkles of *ananda* (bliss) here and there. It's the whole cupcake, not just the icing. But let's be honest—the icing is the best part.

What gives us bliss? Awe, wonder, being in love, being with friends, sharing, laughing, coffee, water when you are so thirsty you can't stand it, crying with joy, Coke, being with a teacher of truth, listening to music, a path of joy, enlightenment, movies, watching, pretending, being silly, letting go, massages, chocolate,

Baby Jesus, Laughing Buddha, cupcakes, cheesecake, steak, etc.

The highest bliss is the source of all these. Whenever we are enjoying them, we disappear into bliss. When we get what we want, the mind, which always searches for the next object of bliss, stops and rests. This resting and dissolving reveals the bliss, which apparently is caused by the object. But it is possible to live from bliss without needing to seek and so that the objects we enjoy are just a bonus. You can enjoy bliss even when you are not eating blueberry cheesecake. It is possible!

How can we rediscover the supreme bliss, which we already *are* yet cannot grasp? The truth is you cannot escape the bliss that you are. By exploring and playing with reality and the facets of silence, we get to have our cake and eat it too. As we let go more and more of our concepts of what we are and surrender into the sublime death of the little me, bliss is what is left over. Bliss is what is left over after the entire universe dissolves. Again, the whole cupcake is bliss!

We sometimes mistake moments of joy that come and go as bliss. These moments are not the same as the permanent, unchanging, unmoving bliss that is the root of all moments of joy. Chasing and grasping happy experiences only gives us a superficial taste of bliss. The objects of reflection in the mirror are not the mirror itself. What is looking at the image in the mirror is the faceless bliss of self. This faceless self is the unknown and sublime death of all concepts. When there is nothing left to hold onto, what remains?

The world is full of bliss, and the root of bliss is unknown. Simply enjoy it.

Holy Spirit

When we are open to a path of joy, the Holy Spirit waits like Batman for the Bat-signal in the sky. Then it swoops down to rescue us from the Joker-mind. How can we turn this signal on? The signal is on right now, but if you turn it off, Batman (the Holy Spirit) could miss you and hit a hot dog stand two miles down the road. Missing you would be a tragedy! The truth is, the Holy Spirit is faster than Batman and can also see much better at night. It is so fast that sometimes it can look as if is standing right beside you before you even think to turn the signal back on.

My first concept of the Holy Spirit (other than hearing it in church) came from *A Course in Miracles*. I was twelve years old and had just moved to Calgary to live with my father. I didn't have a very good relationship with him, or at least I felt I didn't know him well. I always sensed he loved me, but he was simply not in a good emotional/mental space to be there for me in the traditional way.

Before that I was living with my mother and stepfather in St. Albert. I had asked my mother repeatedly if I could go live with my dad. After struggling with the decision, she eventually allowed me to go as a solution to the depression that had been building up inside me. My father, who had been on the dark side for years, was just coming into recovery and making a change for the better. He said no to our request at first but then changed his mind shortly after and said yes.

I moved that year, and then the popcorn effect in my world really started. At the time, my father was big into self-development and spirituality, all of which I had not been exposed to until I arrived. He was into expressing his emotions, doing therapy, reading spiritual books, and watching *Star Trek*. We would often go to the theatre, especially on half-priced Tuesdays (it was $2.50 back then), and we would pig out on popcorn, pop, and goodies. Then we would rent a movie and do the same at home. Thus began my movie and pigging-out addiction.

We basically lived off of pizza (I am not kidding that I ate it every night) and movies. Even when we took a night off from pizza, I would go and grab a pizza sub. I remember having chest pains at the age of twelve, and it was no wonder I had acne, but I digress. My father was a nightmare for me because I had decided to shut down my heart completely, and there he was, Mr. Intense Emotion, yelling, screaming, or crying. It made me feel very uncomfortable.

I had made a decision at a very early age that I would stop feeling emotions because they just got me into nothing but trouble. I would stare at him curiously, thinking, "This guy is so strange—he won't stop expressing his emotions! Doesn't he have any self-control like I do? He's so immature for his age!"

However, this situation was exactly what the Holy Spirit had in mind for the both of us, and it was an interesting and intense dance. Out of love my dad made it his mission to help me release my "repressed emotions." Later on, the idea of always being repressed haunted me as if I were a time bomb waiting to go off. It took me years to get over the idea that I was repressed. Thanks for that one, Dad!

One day I curiously asked him about *A Course in Miracles* because he seemed to be fascinated with it. Through practising the book's lessons, he'd experienced an awakening that had begun to shift his life. In some way, I resonated with his new energy (the popcorn effect). As well, the radiance of a presence out of nowhere was subtly supporting my curiosity about the book. It was a gentle whisper to my heart, a powerfully silent welcoming, and an invitation to the Holy Spirit. It was like a seed (or kernel) from within or an instant suspended in eternity; being had begun to unfold within my awareness.

Out of the eternal moment, in an instant in time while I was alone in the middle of the day, I stared at the book as it lay on the glass coffee table in the middle of the room. Then I eagerly picked it up as if I were Harry Potter. The bookmark was placed in the lesson section, so I turned to one of the lessons. Stillness ensued as I watched my awareness melt into an infinite peace that was so familiar and natural. As I read, "Nothing I see in this room means anything," my little mind opened up into Heaven. It challenged what I had learned up until that moment.

The experience was of an obvious reality brought about by that kernel of truth, a view different from what the world had shown me in my twelve years on planet Earth. There were 365 lessons, one for each day, in which we could rewrite the programmes, judgments, and beliefs we had accepted as our reality... how beautiful. Whatever helps put us on the path of joy, even for an instant, is the Holy Spirit's love and grace and always evokes awe and wonder. It could be meditation, a book, a loving glance, a cup of coffee, or nothing at all. (That's my personal favourite.)

We forget this simple experience of reality, maybe because it is so natural and familiar, or maybe because we slip back into the habitual programming that we have adopted from the world. Whatever the reason, I was soon to forget my experience and continue my life as if asleep to reality, dreaming as we all do a seemingly endless fantasy of changing images leading us in a maze of time. But thank God, reality is real and so powerful that an instant of eternity holds sway over all ego beliefs in time. The mind may get lost, but the heart does not ever forget the ascendant reality of the holy instant—full of Christ, guided by the Holy Spirit, and lived in God.

The emotional ups and downs, fearful idols, painful thoughts, complex ideas, and dramatic displays continued in my life as time went on. I saw fleeting glimpses of peace between the dancing images on the screen of the silence. As if waiting, the Holy Spirit began to have more pull as my heart lost interest in useless pursuits and began searching for lasting peace. I could no longer deny myself, nor live in this world; life seemed to crash into me, making it extremely difficult to live in any sane way.

While questioning my sanity in a moment of confusion, I was moved into the course where the answer was plain. My sanity was found in surrendering to God (whatever that was) in the silence. My perception had begun to be more refined, bringing with it clarity: I realised I would never be full of heart until I permanently experienced reality—perfect peace. I couldn't live without God or I would die.

As reality became clearer to me and the bridge to Heaven closer, my mind became more frustrated. My thoughts and perceptions of reality could not bring me any peace. Engaging my ego for so long as a means of uniting with God had failed. (Failure from the ego's point of view is success in terms of awakening.) Feeling like a failure after wasting years striving for the truth, I gave up, holding nothing. Feeling crushed and facing the humility of not knowing anything, not finding peace, and not being able to help a single person, I surrendered. In one holy instant, I embraced the silence—or rather, the Holy Spirit embraced it for "me." I was unknowing, and like an innocent baby, I had given up all thoughts and opinions as my heart cried out in silence, "If there is a God, help me! I can't do it—I don't know how!" Then there was silence...

The door opened again, just for a sweet instant, as if for a second I was twelve again. Suddenly, I was having the same eternal experience. It was as if the Holy Spirit had been walking beside me all my life, waiting for my mind to cease its constant chatter. Then for a split second of eternity, it rushed in, revealing the path of joy and all the gifts of Heaven.

The Holy Spirit is the sign that the process of enlightenment is apparent only; in reality, it is more like eternal magic. The magic of the Holy Spirit is our ticket to the real show. Similarly, the miraculous popcorn effect is happening right in front of us always. We don't see the show because we are looking every-where but where this magic of the spirit is popping up.

Then it happens—the kind of infinite good that we all sense can be true but seems too good to be true really does happen. Fortunately, belief in it is not required and has nothing to do with it. A door opens for all, an ever-present path through the door into the kingdom of Heaven. The path is so easy and simple that it is overlooked by our complex minds.

The path of joy is an effortless rise beyond limitation to experience the silence any time we choose. Continued exploration of the silence results in the experience of perpetual perfection and awareness of the holy instant. Finally dissolving all barriers, illusions, and separation as the door expands to unity, our awareness becomes infinity expressed in everything— an experience of infinite unity forever unfolding in perfection and bliss.

Did you think we just pop and that's it, game over? The real game is just beginning.

Joy

It's a good day to die.
—Tasunka Witko (Crasy Horse), a holy man of the Lakota

Stop it, you're killing me!
—Laughing Buddha

I used to be depressed and suicidal, but it was the good kind of suicidal because I had a sneaking suspicion that if I killed myself, I would have to come back to the planet I was so desperately trying to escape. This made me even more depressed because I really couldn't kill myself if I wanted to escape. Why had God put me in this terrible position of not wanting to stay but being unable to go? (Later I saw how much I identified with the "I am my body" idea. This identification was the root of the problem.)

This reminds me of a documentary I saw about near-death experiences. A woman had just committed suicide and was floating out of her body when an angel approached her. The angel said to her as she floated up to Heaven, "Hey, we get it— life sucks for you down there, and usually when you're dead, you're dead, and you can't go back. But in your case, we'll give you the option. If you stay here in Heaven, eventually you'll go back in another body but with the same issues. But if you go back now, you can make new choices and perhaps your life will change for the better." The angel orchestra probably started playing the *Jeopardy* theme music as they eagerly awaited her decision. Time's up! She chose to come back. Otherwise how could she have told us about her near-death experience?

It was my hobby to find ways of escaping the pain of my life. I tried escaping through relationships, frappuccinos, drugs (some legal, such as social anxiety medications), and alcohol. When that didn't work, I turned to the many spiritual books and spiritual teachers. Eventually, I became a spiritual addict, spending all my time and money at the local New Age bookstore picking up crystals and the next book I thought was going to give me that enlightenment beam. I saw finding God as my only way out. In some ways it seemed as if I was making progress, but in others I was getting worse.

During a retreat, I kept telling the teacher that I was depressed. He would say, "No, you're not." I kept thinking, "*Yes, I am depressed!* You're not hearing me!" I would get very angry and frustrated. Then one day I was sitting down about seven minutes after I'd just heard the "No, you're not," when something interesting happened. As I was wondering how I was ever going to get rid of that energy, the teacher came over beside me, and dropped a two-litre bottle of Coke, and said, "Here, this should help with your depression!" Wow, it did help instantly. Coke was not a part of the holistic diet at the retreat, and receiving it was like getting a million dollars. It made me forget all about my little self and showed me that "I" was never depressed. Depression was just a story that I could give up. In this case, I gave it up for Coke. What I am, as the stillness, is never depressed.

It's all a matter of interest. What we focus on grows. If I am depressed, it is because I have an interest in being depressed, and as a result, I get self-absorbed. I am not saying that the energy of depression is not there; I am sure it can be, but that is not my point. The point is, if there is interest in depression, then the little "I" identifies with this label. But distract me with something like Coke, and suddenly I lose interest and may even forget that depression is there at all. There is a powerful lesson in that. (Note: offering water won't usually work; if someone comes up to you and says they are depressed and you offer them water, they will just burst into tears. You might as well give them a Kleenex with the water while you're at it—great job, by the way!)

The path of joy is just like opening a bottle of Coke. Instead, it is opening the silence. This is happiness!

When the puppet appears depressed, I am okay with it

because it's just part of the puppet's condition; so what? There is depression, anxiety, or paranoia, but who cares if I'm none of those things in reality? All that exists is energy and whatever label you give it. You could just as easily label anxiety bliss. That's right—anxiety is bliss. Wouldn't it be funny if the things we have been labelling our whole lives were mislabelled? What would happen if you stopped labelling what moves through your body? Find out for yourself!

When observing the movements in my mind, I noticed that the energy would come, and right away I would think, "Oh shit, here it is," and label it as anxiety. Then my mind would go to the past and think, "I've had this anxiety my whole life." Then my mind would go to the future, and I'd wonder, "When will I ever get rid of this anxiety?" You need to see this for yourself; through your own experience, observe what you do with this energy.

I saw my whole process of labelling applied to the past and the future. I would apply it in these directions instantly when the energy labelled "anxiety" came up. As I became familiar with this pattern, which happened in auto-puppet mode, I started to catch it before it took over. Then next time the energy came, I took a moment while I was experiencing it to just watch it innocently without labelling it or thinking of the past or future.

While watching the mind with innocence and without mental commentary, I laughed as I saw that the same energy was infinite joy. It had always been joy my whole life, from childhood right up until that moment. Then I saw how simple it all was. The energy of pure infinite joy moved through a filter of puppet-like, mental programming that I had picked up and identified with. This neutral energy was then transformed into anxiety and fear that over time had been reinforced by the programming. This energy gets stuck in the energetic puppet body, which further strengthens the belief that anxiety is real, creating a virtually inescapable anxiety loop.

It makes perfect sense that this energy was too much to

handle and overwhelming because the pure joy of the popcorn effect was pushing through my programmed filter. The ego cannot control it or manage the energy. All that we can do is get the heck out of the way, and then we are laughing. In other words, by distracting ourselves with the silence, we lose interest in ourselves and our problems.

When I say, "It's a good day to die," people give me the strangest looks. The meaning has been distorted since the Native Indians stopped using it. This saying suggests freedom, peace, fearlessness, and clarity. It says everything about the courageous great spirit we have in the heart. Indians used to say it before battle to pump each other up, giving them strength to face the enemy. This makes sense. Would you want to go to battle if your chief was telling you it was a bad day to die? That kind of negativity would really get you down if you were heading into battle.

Have you ever pretended that today is the last day of your life? How is it for you? You can experience a sense of wonder and joy in the moment (if you are not scared of dying in twenty-three hours and counting down the seconds to your inevitable demise). "It's a good day to die" doesn't say to bring on death—it says to bring on life. It says to live life fully right now, without the fear of death.

Death has a bad rap. But it is part of life; we die all the time, but we associate the word "death" with sadness instead of joy. Death represents the disappearance of everything that would stop us from enjoying life, what we resist that keeps us locked in old patterns. How can that be bad? "It's a good day to die" says, "I allow it—bring it on." Then death becomes a celebration because it is no longer associated with the body but with a change in form. Ultimately, this is a change of form into the formless and the deathlessness of joy.

Will that change of form really matter to us when it is a good day to die? What will I resist when I say yes to it all? Nothing can stop the great spirit that resists nothing and allows everything. "It's a good day to die" means death to our limited self! It's the same as losing yourself in the silence.

You have probably heard of the sage Ramana Maharishi. He is probably the most famous of the recent "enlightened fellows." How did he become enlightened? He died! He didn't do it physically but he went through the death of the little "me" that is attached to the puppet-body.

It started with a fear of death that suddenly popped up, and he started to believe that he was actually going to die. So he lied down to accept and allow the process of death to happen. Talk about extreme pretending. Ironically most of us are pretending to be alive instead of dead. After seeing the whole dissolution and death of the small self, he woke up without the sense of having a separate self. He understood the cosmic joke that the great spirit could not die. He embraced the saying, "It's a good day to die!" He went to battle and saw that there is no battle. He jumped and saw there is no jumper. He died and saw there is no death, only the joy of life.

The truth is that nobody would wake up without death. We have to die! Yippee for death! If it makes you feel better, your puppet doesn't die—it just loses its strings.

Oneness

The Heart, where the Supreme Silence of God's Grace is shining, is the only state of Kaivalyam(supreme oneness), in the presence of which the rare pleasure of all the heavens are revealed to be nothing.

—Sri Muruganar

By holding nothing at all, the stillness, ever revealing, unfolds its natural oneness. A wonderful awe takes hold of our attention, and everything stops as we enjoy the shining brilliance of self. Then amazingly, our attention wanders to the story train as it passes over the oneness, and we are off for another ride. Out of nowhere, and after some time on this train comes the shining awareness—the gift of God. The mind says, "Why did I hop on that story train? Why can I not stay in this oneness? I should be more aware." Yet all this chatter goes unnoticed because we have no interest in it. A wonderful thoughtless attitude arises that can only be translated as *"Who cares?"* There is instant gratitude at the gift of attention. The miracle is not taken for granted, and now we are in love. The beloved captures our awareness, and no story train, plane, automobile, or roller skates make any difference to us at all. All we are left with is this gift that the angels have given to awaken us into supreme oneness.

What does it mean to be one? What does an enlightened sage experience when she looks at a tree? Oneness or non-duality happens when everything is taken away. In the silence there are no concepts of oneness. There are no concepts of duality or non-duality, so what is left to be seen?

The phrase *neti-neti* (not this, not this) beautifully reflects that it is impossible to describe oneness other than to say it is not what we think it is. The path of joy is about our direct experience of oneness. We can share this oneness energetically and even in words, but it is beyond the intellect's understanding. We are oneness, yet the mind exists in the realm of multiplicity. Once we are content with not knowing (non-conception), what remains will become self-evident. It is the silence.

We are already resting in the supreme oneness as we seek it, in all directions. It is too close to exist in any direction other than here—right above your nose in the space you are looking out of. This space goes infinitely inwards and outwards, yet in the silence, neither inner nor outer exists.

In the silence, there is no concept of you. In the nothingness, where seeing happens, there is no separate individual, only silence. In the nothingness, there is no concept of a tree. There is nothing. There is no concept of "other" in the silence. What is the essence of the tree without the concept? What is the essence of me and you without the concept or the mental images we project?

When nothing is there, how can we quantify what we are? This is supreme oneness without end. Explore it, and immediately discover that you are it. This is the ultimate way of the sage that leads to the popcorn effect. This popping increases exponentially as one touches this oneness. All it takes is one.

Unity

There is no becoming (creation), destruction, bondage, desire
to sever (bondage), effort (made for liberation) for those who
have attained (liberation). Know that this is the supreme truth
(Paramartha)!
—Ramana Maharishi

After I found the practice and a teacher who changed my life, I
experienced an epiphany. I had thought that through trial and
error I had been guided to the completion of my journey, but in
reality it had nothing to do with my choices but with impersonal
unity.

My story was the effect of unity; unity was not the result of my
story. This is the magic of grace: whatever happens in the story,
the unity of God is the underlying primal motivator. Our stories
vary in a million different ways yet are really only a beautiful
painting on the canvas of silence.

Unity is way too advanced for anybody because there isn't
anybody. Nobody will achieve it because there is nobody. It
happens for no one. That is the end of the story. Sorry to give
away the ending, but it's better than I make it sound.

Nobody gets enlightened or has ever been enlightened. It only
looks that way from the perspective of separation from unity.
That perspective of separation, however, is also happening in
unity.

How complicated is unity? How complicated is *one*?

In order for you to get enlightened, there would have to be at
the very least the two objects, you and enlightenment. That
duality does not exist in the experiencing of oneness. Now you
can relax because you will never be free. Isn't it wonderful news
that the struggle is over?

There is only unity. I have been telling stories of a path to
unity and a process. This is the story of awakening. There are

millions of them going on as we speak. Just go to a New Age bookstore and you will find many of them. None of them are true. Nobody has ever achieved the goal of unity. Nobody has left unity. Unity is all there is.

Why even bother with it all? Who is bothering with it? Can you stop the quest? Even trying to stop the quest is happening in unity. There is no escape. That is the wonderful secret to it all. This is the cause for causeless joy, the reason to laugh for no reason at all. How can you fail the quest when there is no you and no quest? You are already unity. Cue cosmic laughter!

The fact that we are already free now is the perfect expression of love. This is how far away we are from the truth. All of this is a joke. What can we do about it? Nothing. As they say in show business, "The show must go on." The story must continue and will only appear to come to an end when the shift into unity happens. When it happens, you are not there as a concept of you but as the *big you*. This shift is only part of the story, however. The shift happens for unity.

If we journey far enough back into the past, before the birth of identification with the sense of self and the body and before the birth of the universal story, we end in unity. If we travel into the future after the death of identification with the sense of self and the body and after the dissolution of the universal story, there is nothing but unity.

Within unity arises the story of awakening. There are actually four phases in unity: unity, auto-puppet, awakening, and unity. It is a unity sandwich. Unity is eternally sandwiching itself between the salami and mustard story in between. This is happening in this eternal moment now. All of us are sandwiched. Some are stuck in the middle, some have slipped off to the side, and the rest ate the sandwich, leaving only crumbs.

Then we have the story of after-puppet unity. (That could be another state of consciousness—I just make them up as we go.) In this phase, the puppet does not disappear, only its separate owner. It continues as part of the story, but we no longer identify with it. The puppet is now harmlessly in the arms of the great puppet master.

The salami and mustard auto-puppet/awakening story is happening within this eternal unity sandwich, which is actually more like a wrap; being fully loaded, it folds in on itself. Without this unity-wrap of silence, the story of awakening would not be possible. The story just makes this unity-wrap interesting because otherwise, it would look like a thin, tortilla shell to the mind.

I don't know about you, but I am getting super hungry. Who wants tacos? (This is a literal question, not an existential one.)

The Zen of How

The first and most important question is, "What do you want more than anything?" We are very blessed when we know what we want because our focus will ensure we stay on track. The answer to this question will bring us back to the path when we are wandering off or feeling scattered or confused. Clarity about what we want is important because if we don't know where to set our compass, we could end up at the North Pole instead of relaxing on the beach. Do you know what they call a monkey at the North Pole? Lost.

Moving toward peace, freedom, bliss, fulfillment, and love all lead to the same destination. When there is freedom, there is peace. When you have fulfillment, you have bliss. Just pick one because each one will lead to the next, and all these roads lead to silence.

After we know what we want, there is a second question that is not absolutely necessary but very useful if we are going to arrive at the beach instead of the North Pole. It is a time saver, if you will. You may say, "Sure, I get it—there is only unity. But what can I do to get where I'm going?" The next question, then, is about the Zen of how. How do I get what I want? The simple answer is by exploring the stillness.

When I asked the teacher, "What do I do?" the response was, "Lose yourself in the silence and don't think at all." How do I do that, you ask? You jump on the path of joy to directly experience what stillness is.

The path of joy is synonymous with the path of the sages, which actively engages the stillness now. Regardless of what path you are on, you can master not taking yourself seriously. This is a path of joy, and believe it or not, not taking yourself seriously is how to pop into freedom.

How can you and I know that not taking anything seriously will lead to freedom? By testing it out! Be a cosmic explorer. You will never know for sure unless you walk the walk. Only something separate can take things seriously. The stillness can focus on objects, but it cannot take them seriously since they keep changing shape. Ultimately, every problem of identification comes from a distorted interest in taking it seriously.

By starting to laugh at these things, they lose the seriousness that giving them attention leads to, and they fall away. Eventually, the only thing left to not take seriously is *you*, and then you are really laughing your way home. The path of joy is the absolute path that engulfs you in a sea of eternal bliss.

Start by picking one thing a day to take less seriously, until there is nothing left. When you take everything away, what is left? Find out, and you become popcorn for God.

How exactly does a path of joy dissolve separation? The first step on the path of joy is discerning the real from the false. We touched on this process earlier. The silence without movement is the underlying reality. On a path of joy, only silence can awaken us from what is not real. The path of joy is not a religion, belief, or series of concepts. It is the end of concepts. What you think you are is a product of your concepts. But what you are is concept-less, free of concepts. The goal of a path of joy is to dissolve concepts, leaving only what is left—the surprise of the popcorn effect.

Separation is the last thing to dissolve because it is the root concept of all the other concepts. It stands to reason that if not taking things seriously dissolves concepts, then eventually you will be laughing at the biggest concept of all: being a separate part of the whole.

A path of joy does nothing to you to make you more whole. It simply removes concept after concept until there is only the concept-less wholeness of what is.

This is how a path of joy works! Whether it happens right now or a thousand lives from now makes no difference to stillness. It only matters to the one who appears to be separate.

This is again the incredible importance of the Zen of how!

What are the signs you are on the path of joy?

You are always being directed to the silence.

Practising is fun, easy, and simple if you don't take it seriously.

If your journey to the path of joy takes the form of a technique such as meditation or a teaching of some kind, these must lead to stillness. If they lead to a concept, you are on something other than a path of joy. A concept changes, but the stillness does not.

If we experience a problem on the path, we can't blame the teaching. We have evidence of what works best based on our experience, and we must be thinking and taking ourselves seriously if we are having problems.

What if what we are practising does not work after we give it a good chance (a couple of months of commitment)? Before you decide to try something else, consider the following:

Stay open to the possibility that your mind might be making the path more difficult that it is. Remember to stay innocent and don't take yourself and your practice seriously. Commitment and focus are important, but not seriousness.

Ask the experts. Talk to those who are masters at the meditation, practice, or path you have chosen. Stay open to their advice because they have experience. There is always someone with greater experience and wisdom than you possess, and only the ego will not want to ask for help. People can stay stuck "doing it the hard way" for years. Don't be like this. Be open to ease and advice that works. Trust your teachers and fellow cosmic explorers.

Trust yourself. If your gut tells you no, don't force it. This is about enjoyment. On a path of joy, meditation is enjoyable and addictive. The stillness is addictive! You don't do it because you have to; you do it because you can't wait. It is exciting! It's the greatest mystery and adventure of all time. If it is not enjoyable, don't waste your time.

Exploring what you are is fun and exciting, and if what you practise is not giving you joy, then perhaps it is time to move on. Meditation is not manipulation of any kind; it is natural.

What happens if you keep falling off the path? What do you do? Join the club! I have fallen off the path thousands of times. One time I fell completely off the mountain, but that is an embarrassing story I don't want to relive right now. Let's just say I had my tail between my legs.

Falling off the path is natural, as we are only human, and we have our habits. Recommit to the practice. A path of joy will always provide an effortless and direct means back to the silence. And if we have the right tools for the job, returning will not take long.

The path of joy provides us with tools to assist us on the journey so that we have the twenty-four hours a day choice to attend to our true nature. There are no side effects on the path of joy, only a release of stress. On the path of joy, we have support from the silence, fellow cosmic explorers, and teachers. These teachers are not more advanced than we are; they do the same thing we do, so we are all in the same boat. But they do have experience in exploring the silence and allowing, which can be useful for us. Take advantage of them. Ask questions about your practice. Remember that consciousness unfolds most quickly through play. Playing with your fellow cosmic explorers and playing with the silence are the keys to freedom. We are all here to play. We are all doing it anyway; we just don't see it that way.

There are many paths out there including no path at all. Some are more efficient that others. If you are on a path that works for you, terrific! You are one of the lucky ones. If you haven't found what you are looking for, keep exploring and trying new things. The universe will give you what you need. If you are really lazy and just want something right now, then I recommend learning what my friends and I practise.

The Bright Path is a focused and simple teaching. My favourite thing about it is that it works. It is simple because it always directs our attention to what is real. We can call this the ascendant, the infinite, divinity, God, silence, or even the super-dazzling, radiant, all-shining, brilliant Self. We have different concepts about this one thing or "no-thing," but the experience of this silence is simple.

The Bright Path gives us what we need to easily experience the fullness of life. Very quickly we start to understand how little we really need to do to have it all. We spend our lives trying to achieve all the things outside us that we feel are important. We struggle to achieve them because we think they will bring us joy and a sense of completion. Even when we get what we want, it never gives us the fulfillment we were looking for, so we keep searching for the next thing on the list. That we are never satisfied is a good thing; it means that God has something greater in store for us than temporary happiness. Peace and freedom are important, and enlightenment becomes our highest desire. How do we get all that good stuff?

Our attention has been focused on what we wanted to achieve and the effort to get it (the effort of "mini me"). The Bright Path techniques take that effort and attention and leave us with effortless attention. The universe, God, and the angels all know our passion. The fire in the heart "to know" is enough. The Bright Path teaches us to gently rest and allow the inevitable to unfold. The effortlessness of reality takes over. Our experience is complete and is already everything we want. So what is the problem?

The problem is always mental. A fantasy in the mind appears. It is a product of our imagination, yet we believe it is real. Why? We are dreaming in a dream—thinking, fantasising, and imagining. But what is wrong with dreaming? Absolutely nothing! The first praise technique of The Bright Path addresses the sense that "something is wrong with this dream." By using the praise technique, we are lifted right out of auto-puppet mode into a direct experience of the stillness. The best part is that it is mechanical and automatic.

The teachings of The Bright Path help you to wake up from the dream, but not because your dream is bad—only because you want to wake up. The silence allows the dream to be whatever it is. The only thing that wants to change it is the mind, which is a dream as well.

Here are some important questions. Is the attention on the dream or on reality? How can I focus my attention on reality?

The reason God hasn't appeared in your dream and said, "Hey, what the heck are you doing? You're messing your dream up—you need to take charge and change it a little," is because God does not care what you do in your dream. (Plus I hear he is very busy right now.) The unconditional love of the silence is really *that* unconditional. It simply allows you to be you—good, bad, or ugly, and with a happy dream or a sad dream. So who can we blame?

Personally, I like to blame consciousness because that is what fell asleep in the first place. Or maybe I could blame Narain (the cosmic dreamer), who created all this mess by dreaming. I used to think it was very unfair that the infinite didn't care about my problems. Then in one moment, I realised that there are no problems in reality; problems appear only in the separate dream story.

I was identifying with the thoughts in my head. I was in dream mode, then I woke up, then I fell asleep, and so on, just dreaming and waking up. It wasn't until I found The Bright Path that I could say I had any real choice in the matter. It is so empowering and reassuring to know that if I am taking my dream seriously, I have techniques available twenty-four hours a day to instantly and effortless remember reality or to move toward it. Even an intense hurricane of energy cannot stop the inward movement into the joy and freedom of what is.

The Teacher and the Teaching

My first introduction to the path of joy came on Valentine's Day weekend in 1999. I met my meditation teacher during that weekend course in Vancouver in which the techniques of The Bright Path were given. Later on, he became much more than just my meditation teacher. The relationship became about the silence, of which he said, "Ninety-nine per cent of this relationship is in the silence."

During that weekend, he said, "You are going to experience what all saints and sages have experienced throughout all time and space." When he said it, my heart was pounding hard with excitement and for no reason (other than that I was in resonance with stillness). I had no doubt that I was about to experience what I had longed for in the heart. My mind had no idea what that would be. There was conviction in his words. As well, something powerfully energetic and unknown was happening in the room. This weekend was not about him—it was about me, the other eighteen students, and the teaching we were being exposed to. It was about what we wanted more than anything.

This was and is the teaching of the one. No belief is required, just the direct experience of the non-dual infinite. The infinite is all there is, and we are already that. If everybody could see that or rather *be* that, then there would be no more seeking. All the seminar and course-jumping would stop. One of the popular ads at the time for the meditation was: "The search is over." To me, that summed up the course. Unfortunately, I did not stop seeking, but hey, I'm only human. At least I had the choice now.

What happened to make us forget the infinite?

As soon as I was introduced to the first technique, I remembered the path of joy. Even though the weekend was pure bliss and a coming home, I was determined to do it on my own. I had many reasons to do it by myself. After all, I had been preparing for this for years. Best of all, I had the tools to take me to the depths of being.

I had been looking for a teacher and perhaps a teaching that fit my image of what enlightenment looked like (based on what I'd read and heard). Many years had already passed before I found what I'd been looking for all along. It happened during that weekend, yet I was not willing to give up seeking. The addictive energy of looking for God outside myself kept me wandering. Looking back, I see that it was only a matter of time before I exhausted myself by struggling and thinking. My efforts had an expiration date, but God let me keep on fooling myself for a time.

After meeting the teacher who reconnected me with the ancient and fresh path of joy and being taught the techniques of The Bright Path, I decided to pack my bags and go find enlightenment in India. God has a funny sense of humour. I remember the silent laughter resonating in my heart as I sat on the concrete floor listening to the *oms* and waiting for my teacher to show up in the ashram. The laughter said, "You didn't need to come all this way, but since you did, enjoy the sights, sounds, and cows."

Armed with the techniques that gave me everything, I went out on a mission, seeking three of the most enlightened teachers I could find to tap me with the enlightenment stick. (They needed superpowers for sure.) And I wanted to check to see if I could find anything better than the meditation techniques I had just learned. I went to the holiest of places with books and techniques, and I went to town experimenting with it all.

Even when I knew in my heart that I had made a connection with the teaching, I declined an invitation to a six-month retreat. To be honest I really wanted the honour and credit of having done it myself, the "right way." Never underestimate the ego's arrogance in thinking it can do without help. After all, I was very special, and my story was way too important to be ignored. I had invested so much of my energy in the story of my awakening that I didn't want to stop, even when I'd found everything I was looking for. The universe must have been shaking its head in disgust.

I didn't find enlightenment in India, although I did meet some very nice swamis and yogis, and I did encounter some helpful teachings. I was searching for a jewel that I had in my pocket the whole time. The Bright Path was the jewel that led me to what I wanted—a deep and intimate connection with the silence.

After God got frustrated with me and I went through a couple of cults for some deep cleansing (punishment), I returned home with a new perspective: I would make money. (Anything was better than trying to destroy the ego.) The cults, quite frankly, weren't very nice, but hey, we sometimes do strange things to get free food. At least I'd learned what I didn't want my path to be. Thank God I had experienced the original innocence and an effortless way to freedom.

Sometimes we need to put our hand in the fire to know it's hot. I was even told not to do it, but like an idiot I did it anyway. I had a bad habit of not listening to good advice out of arrogance. When I went to San Miguel, Mexico, a friend of mine said, "Whatever you do, don't eat from the street vendors. You will get sick!" What did I do? When I got off the bus, I grabbed some food from the street. I was arrogant enough to think that I could handle it. I was terribly ill for days and praying to die. Why did I keep doing stupid things like that? So many times my mind would ignore simple, good advice. Was I wired to put my hand in the fire? Was I wired for stupidity? I had my reasons.

While working in Calgary one day, I had a moment of reflection. (Some people call that thinking.) I looked at my future, split in two directions: a nice condo and a nice bank account versus pursuing and obtaining freedom. Based on my "brilliance," I decided that logically it made more sense to go for freedom because the choices I would make from that space would be better and for the highest good. I would have gone that way anyway, but I thought I needed to come up with a noble reason to go for it.

I knew the meditation teacher I'd met in Vancouver had something that I wanted. I knew it from the way he'd looked at me when I said, "Does this really work? Because let me tell you, I have so much anxiety, it would make a cat spasm to death." I still don't know what happened in that moment, but nobody had ever looked at me like that, and my sense of self felt uncomfortable in my body. He just gazed at me and said nothing. I was thinking, "This is weird," but internally something was registering, as if he knew something that wasn't clear to me. Energetically, it felt as if he was looking right through me.

A seed had been planted. Even though I denied it and ignored it for years by searching on my own, it was later revealed as the underlying reality of everything, including the unbearable yearning to be united with that reality. Recognising that connection, I acknowledged my belief that I could successfully bring about my own awakening was false and that I had failed. With this failure came an immeasurable bliss and relief. Although failure had been written on my face many times, this time I was indeed defeated and had to face the inevitable unknown. I packed my bags and went for the retreat to get the whole enchilada.

Slowly, the innocence and humility of the environment started to rub off on me, challenging my yogi-wannabe nature. I was surrounded by monks whom I expected at any moment to point at me and aggressively show me my ego. That never happened.

Instead, I was left open and willing for the teaching of the one to flow into my stubborn mind. But I would resist and struggle. My programming and conditioning was strong. My fears were overwhelming me as I over-pondered what I was doing. I was thinking intensely when Maharishi came to me and said, *"Thinking disturbs your bliss. You don't need to think anymore."*

That was the only key I needed to hear on this path of joy. If we could all forgo thinking on our own, we would all be free of pain and suffering. However, most of us don't, which is why out of grace and love, we find ourselves with all the universal support we need. Hopefully, we don't run the other way out of fear.

I had the great honour of spending the six-month retreat in British Columbia and went completely inward. I had the opportunity to spend time with many amazing teachers from around the world. Each had wonderful experiences of silence to share. All of them seemed to see me only in my perfection. Never once did they point out anything wrong or to try to challenge or kill my ego. In fact, the ego was never even acknowledged as being real or even talked about much. Instead, all the attention was on what was real and how to experience that. This type of intense focus consumed time as if it were a piece of newspaper that had been thrown in a fire. This made it easy.

Somehow I got chosen to be the official coffee maker for Maharishi and the team that was helping to run the programme. This was a very cruel job for me since, as students, we were not allowed coffee during the retreat, and I had to smell that amazing smell every day. We were told that drinking caffeine raises the metabolism when meditating, but I think they just didn't want to share.

I never saw Maharishi take anything as seriously as he did coffee. One time someone tapped me on the shoulder and said, "Maharishi wants to see you right now." As my old fears of authority came up, I thought, "Oh shit, what did I do?" I walked up the stairs nervously. He said, "Did somebody use the grinder?" I replied that I didn't think so. Frowning and looking disgusted, he said, "My coffee tastes like French vanilla!" I checked, and sure enough somebody had used French vanilla beans in the grinder; it ruined the special stash he had procured from Nelson, BC. If you are a coffee connoisseur, you will understand how Maharishi felt. At my workplace, the unspoken rule is to never mess with a man's coffee.

I had very specific instructions as a coffee maker — five scoops only and no other beans. Later I was invited to join the team on a retreat in Mexico. I like to think it was because I was enlightened, but probably it was because I kept making Maharishi laugh, and he trusted my coffee-making abilities.

I got to spend a lot of time with him during the next few years, but some of my favourite moments were when I would get up early to start brewing the coffee. I would knock on his door and say "Buenos días, señor!" He would come out with his hair standing straight up. He would sit in silence, staring as if waiting to be activated by some unknown force, and then *pop!* As soon as he had a sip of coffee, he would start telling a story. At other times, we wouldn't speak a word.

Every moment was sacred and alive with the teaching of *one*. I felt as if I was being sucked into the core of stillness. I felt like the luckiest guy in the whole world, especially when I reflected on where I had come from. Never would I take for granted that relationship. It wasn't about him or me. It wasn't about what was said. It was and is the pure love of God, love of the silence, and the path of joy. There is only silence, and in that there is *one*.

"No teacher or no student" says that there is only oneness and that is it. There only appears to be a separate character who needs to wake up. This is the oneness appearing as a non-awake person. But there is only oneness, so oneness wakes itself up in this relationship. In other words, the teacher and student are one. The teacher sees, and the student does not. Oneness appears to both see and not see. Both characters are appearing in oneness. There must be students for the teacher to be a teacher. Otherwise a teacher of oneness would be bored to death with no one to play with.

I remember Maharishi telling a story about waking up one morning and realising there is no teaching. So he said, "I am done with teaching because I have realised there is no teaching."

Then the phone rang with people wanting to take the meditation course. "I guess there is teaching," he said.

I love this story because it says so much about how things actually are despite our revelations of truth. I know we learned that truth is not about belief, but I suspect that beliefs still have an impact even though we are more advanced at popping now.

This teaching is a Happy Meal. It has both a path and no path at all. It is everything and nothing. It helps us see the infinite for ourselves, which refines our self-expression naturally, and puts tools in our hands to help humanity. What else could we possibly want?

What will we be like after we wake up? What will change? Let me give you a hypothetical example.

In Mexico, Eduardo climbs a coconut tree to get coconuts to feed his family. On the way up, he recognises that there is no separate Eduardo and that there is only this freedom. Waking up happens. What does he do? Let go of the tree because it's all an illusion, including his family? He probably continues to climb the tree and get the coconuts because that is what is happening. He continues to do what is in his nature to do. Probably not much will change in his life other than that the popcorn effect will be more active. The waking up had nothing to do with him as a person. It just happened.

This reminds me of the quote, "Before enlightenment chop wood and carry water; after enlightenment chop wood and carry water." The character does what is in his nature to do once he is no longer fascinated with the story. Then what happens is the story turns into what *A Course in Miracles* refers to as a "happy dream."

In my story, the sense of my being in charge has come and gone. It drove my need to ensure "I got it." It ensured that I did my meditation correctly. I was terribly scared that if I wasn't there, I wouldn't get what I wanted.

After letting go of control, I lived what had been my ultimate fear: not knowing how I was doing or where I was on the scale of consciousness. This was not confusion, however; it was nobody there to care. In that enjoyment of silence was a certainty and a clear reflection from the universe that wasn't needed but welcomed as part of the play.

There is only oneness, the shape it takes, and how it shapes our life. We appear to be in charge and then surrender. Fortunately, the teacher is in great shape, holding the silence for us until we remember. The teacher teaches us to rely on the infinite as we gently skip down The Bright Path home.

I guess this is it; I am running out of thoughts. Besides, on my computer I have 108 pages, which is a sacred number in our tradition, so it's a good time to quit. It has been a pleasure to share my thoughts with you, and I hope you enjoyed it.

To conclude, I will share with you a moment I had during a retreat. I couldn't stop thinking, and I had so many ideas that I could not find any peace. I kept running up and down the stairs to see the teacher to empty my bucket of concepts, and he kept saying lose yourself in the silence and no thinking at all. The bucket just kept filling up. Still thinking too much, I came running up the stairs to share. As I was heading back, I got totally frustrated and angry with my mind, and out of nowhere I heard myself say, "There sure are a lot of things *not* to think about."

There you have it—there *are* lots of things *not* to think about. Think about it! Just kidding. Keep emptying the bucket, and I will see you in the silence!

Appendix: The Brahman Stories

Brahman (Silence)

Whether real or unreal, whether knowledge or ignorance gathered by the intellect, whether pleasant or unpleasant to the mind, all are only Brahman and nothing else.
—Sri Muruganar

The Path of Joy is a direct line to Brahman. There is no escaping Brahman. Everything is Brahman. That which is reading these words now is Brahman. The thought that pretends to be separate and hides Brahman is Brahman. That which judges and feels separate is Brahman. That which is, is Brahman. Brahman is nothing and everything. No exceptions and no escape, Brahman is all.

Even that Witch is also Brahman.

Brahman is a name of a type of cow in Mexico. Also it is a name of the infinite Self, Silence or Ascendant. Okay, it's pretty much the name and essence of everything.

In the beginning, there was only Brahman, and everything was called Brahman, but Brahman realised that at dinner time, it became challenging to get what Brahman wanted: "Brahman can you pass the Brahman?" Sometimes Brahman would get salt and other times hot sauce. This began to frustrate Brahman. It started with condiments, then later it spread to Brahman, "the person." To distinguish between Brahman the "frustrated" and Brahman the "just this" Brahman, names were formed. Hence the more "advanced" language that we see in today's society was formed out of that convenience.

It started innocently enough with the duality of salt and hot sauce and then... spread like wild fire into all the names and forms we see today; even our Brahman thoughts and feelings have turned into "the bad" and "the good" instead of that which is Brahman.

Pass the Brahman Please... NO I SAID BRAHMAN!!!

Wonder Ant

That (Brahman) is the whole (purnam); this (the world appearance) is also the whole. Even when (this) whole merges into (that) whole, it is the whole. Even when (this) whole goes out (as if a separate reality) from (that) whole, the whole alone remains.

—Sri Muruganar

This story is based on actual events.

Once upon a time, there was only Brahman. Like a playful child splashing in a puddle of water, and for no reason at all, Brahman made a wave. Since there was only Brahman, Brahman made a Brahman wave. Both waves looked at each other and then laughed as only one wave. Brahman loved making waves so much that there was no stopping him. Like a leaping frog full of caffeine and sugar, Brahman splashed and jumped, making wave after wave.

Many years later, in the infinite "Brahmiverses" was a tiny space very far away. This space was one of the doorways to a whole universe in space-time. Inside it were 10,000 suns and planets. One of those planets was a beautiful sapphire blue, just like the third eye. The closer you got to the blue sphere, the better you could see mountains of green and oceans of blue. Thousands of civilisations were living in all kinds of environments on this sphere. Of the many creatures in this place, the most obvious were the busy giants called "whomans." Nobody knows what or why the whomans were doing what they were doing, or even where they were going, but they each seemed to know with confidence.

Nearer to the centre of the sphere was a small park with many thousands of other kinds of creatures different from the busy whomans. The closer you came to this centre, the more worlds within worlds you could see.

One day while travelling in the park, I witnessed thousands of busy, wandering creatures called wander ants. Just like the strange whomans, they were doing things I didn't understand. Thousands were carrying pieces of green leaves up and down a massive tree. The bright green leaves flickered and sparkled in the sun like a fancy light show.

One of those wander ants was very curious and out of the blue asked another ant, "What is the purpose of this? Why am I here?" "Just do your dance, you wander ant," said the other one. But a bright fire burned in the heart of this wander ant; it was curious and had no choice but to find out all the answers. After tormenting many of the other wander ants for the answers, it was lead by a fellow ant into a party. The ants there had the same passion and curiosity as the wander ant. They were called fire ants because of their burning passion to know truth. It was a contagious passion, and once you were bitten by the fire ants, it was "game over." At least the wander ant felt more at home with this renegade group of fire ants that had given up everything to know the truth.

One evening as the wander ant and the fire ants sat around a fire, the great sage fire ant, who had fierce, squinting eyes and a long white shimmering goatee flowing from his bright red face, spoke these wise words to the curious ant: "Hey, wander ant, if you want to know the truth, you have to wonder within yourself and stop wandering outside yourself like all the wander ants on this sphere!"

All the attentive little ants became very alert and quiet as they wondered within. The wander ant became a wonder ant, and his curiosity had been transformed into a huge energy ball and a fury of silent exploration. Ascending the park in the night, the little ant went higher and higher, past the blue sphere and out past the 10,000 suns into the tiny space, leaving space-time and going out into the many Brahmiverses. The ant went so high as to wander right up to the great Brahman of all that is.

As soon as the wonder ant opened his eyes, he recognised Brahman meditating. He was sitting in the form of an old frog in lotus position with a black baseball hat that had the words "THE BOSS" in bright white. The little ant said loudly, "Wow, this inward-wondering stuff really works. Hello, I am just a wondering ant looking for some answers. Do you have any for me?" Brahman did not move, and he sat still with eyes closed in deep meditation.

All of a sudden, the wonder ant became aware that there were thousands of silent frogs dressed in white robes all around him. All of them were engaged in a profound and silent meditation. The ant, thinking he was disturbing this sacred space somehow and feeling small, was also being filled up with the sacred presence of silence. A little embarrassed at being so loud, the ant began to struggle to get his tiny legs into lotus position. He wanted to show his respect for this amazing group of beings, but his legs were too tiny for his elongated body. He kept falling over and making strange noises to get into position.

The Brahman frog opened one eye slightly, and a big smile formed across his face. At the same time, beside him a frog with a huge belly started to laugh uncontrollably. His laugh was so strange and loud as it broke the silence that it caused all the other frogs to giggle and move up and down in unison. Before the wonder ant knew it, all the frogs were laughing. Some were even falling over as they lost it completely.

The little ant smiled and laughed as all his wondering turned into wonder. Bowing down and giggling like a baby, he brought his tiny ant hands together to show his love for his new frog family. To his amazement, what he saw before his cosmic eyes were the hands of a free frog. He had been a Brahman frog all along.

The Beginning

Bibliography

Glen Ellen. A Course in Miracles. Foundation for Inner Peace, 1992.

Daniel H. Pink. Drive. Riverhead Press, 2009.

Sri Muruganar. *Guru Vachaka Kovai* (The Collection of Guru's Sayings) Translation by Sri Sadhu Om. Sri ArunachalaRamana Nilayam, 2005. Translation by Swami Prabhavananda and Frederick Manchester. The Upanishads. Vedanta Press, 1975.

Visit Paramananda at:
www.paramanandaishaya.com
To learn more about The Bright Path visit:
www.thebrightpath.com

MANTRA
BOOKS

We publish books on Eastern religions and philosophies.
Books that aim to inform and explore the various
traditions, that began rooted in East and
have migrated West.